China's Future

China's Future

David Shambaugh

polity

First published in 2016 by Polity Press
Reprinted 2016 (nine times), 2017 (four times), 2018

Polity Press
65 Bridge Street
Cambridge CB2 1UR, UK

Polity Press
350 Main Street
Malden, MA 02148, USA

ISBN-13: 978-1-5095-0713-9
ISBN-13: 978-1-5095-0714-6(pb)

A catalogue record for this book is available from the British Library.

Library of Congress Cataloging-in-Publication Data

Names: Shambaugh, David L.
Title: China's future / David Shambaugh.
Description: First edition. | Malden, MA : Polity, 2016. | Includes
    bibliographical references and index.
Identifiers: LCCN 2015037154| ISBN 9781509507139 (hardback) | ISBN
    9781509507146 (paperback) | ISBN 9781509507160 (mobi)
Subjects: LCSH: China--Politics and government--2002- | China--Economic
    conditions--2000- | China--Social conditions--2000- | China--Foreign
    relations--21st century.
Classification: LCC DS779.4 .S45 2016 | DDC 951.06--dc23 LC record available at http://
lccn.loc.gov/2015037154

Typeset in 10 on 16.5pt Utopia Std by
Servis Filmsetting Ltd, Stockport, Cheshire
Printed and bound in the United States by LSC Communications

For further information on Polity, visit our website:
politybooks.com

Dedicated to Harry Harding

Contents

List of Figures

Acknowledgments

This book has its origins in a keynote lecture I gave in July 2014 at the "China at the Crossroads" Conference at the Contemporary China Research Center of Victoria University in Wellington, New Zealand. Trying to think through the totality of China and its future trajectory for that event was a challenge, but it percolated in my brain over the subsequent year. During this time I took advantage of invitations to lecture—at the American Academy in Berlin, the University of Edinburgh, the School of Oriental and African Studies at the University of London, and several universities in the United States—to further refine my thinking and revise the lecture. I am most grateful to professional colleagues, students, and members of the audiences for pushing me further in my thinking about China's current state and potential future directions.

As I revised the lecture many times for successive events, I kept wondering what else I could do with the material. It is, after all, one thing for a scholar to give a lecture speculating on the sensitive subject of China's future, but quite another to go into print on it. What turned the material from a lecture into this book came to me one evening just as I finished reading Joseph S. Nye's *Is the American Century Over?* As I marveled at the compact nature (physically and intellectually) of Nye's latest book, it suddenly dawned on me that the lecture I had been giving could be fleshed out into a similar short volume. So I shot Joe an email inquiring about his experience publishing with Polity Press. He responded quickly and very positively, putting me in touch with Louise Knight, the Politics and International Relations editor at Polity. It did not take long for me to elucidate the idea with Louise in emails and a transoceanic phone conversation before she signed me up with a contract for this volume. I am very impressed by the quality of Polity's publications list and the *niche* they have carved out in the market with short and topical books that examine key issues of the day. The idea of writing a relatively short book about China's future appealed to me (despite the daunting nature of the subject). All of my previous books gestated—through research and writing—for about five years each. This one I wrote over eight weeks during the summer of 2015! Once again I was fortunate to retire to our cabins in northern Michigan overlooking Grand Traverse Bay, the perfect place to think and write. I am deeply grateful to my family—my wife Ingrid and sons Christopher and Alexander—for their patience and tolerance as I wrote during vacation time.

I also wish to thank the Smith Richardson Foundation, and particularly Senior Vice-President and Director of Programs Marin Strmecki, for a grant (SRF Grant #2015-0941) to support the research and writing of this book. This is the third of my books that the foundation has supported, for which I am truly grateful. I also wish to thank my home institution—the Elliott School of International Affairs at The George Washington University—for a Strategic Opportunities for Academic Research (SOAR) award. The Elliott School has now been my professional home for two decades, and I am most grateful for the collegial community and research support it has provided.

I also wish to particularly thank my colleagues and friends Bob Ash, Pieter Bottelier, Bruce Dickson, Tom Gold, Chris Horner, David Lubin, Andrew Nathan, Bob Sutter, and Michael Yahuda for taking the time to read individual draft chapters. Their expertise helped much to substantively improve the manuscript and save me from embarrassing errors. I also wish to thank Ann Klefstad for her excellent copyediting of the manuscript, while Louise Knight, Nekane Tanaka Galdos, and Neil de Cort at Polity Press have all been a true pleasure to work with throughout the publication process.

Finally, I wish to dedicate this volume to Harry Harding. He and I first met in 1978 and have been close friends and colleagues ever since. While I was not his student, Harry mentored me from afar during my graduate school years and offered me important academic opportunities. If he had not been supportive of my application for a scholarship to go to China to conduct my doctoral dissertation research, I would not have been selected and thus likely would never have had an academic career. He "rescued" me at a critical juncture in my graduate education. Subsequently, Harry also became my Dean and faculty colleague at George Washington University's Elliott School of International Affairs, after he lured me back across the Atlantic from England where I was then resident and teaching. We have remained in close contact since he decamped from GWU to go to the University of Virginia and Hong Kong University of Science and Technology. We share the same areas of professional interest and expertise—China, Asia, and U.S.-China relations—and have interacted in countless conferences on these topics over the years. I have always marveled at Harry's extraordinary intellectual ability to incisively analyze a problem or an issue, and to place it in a larger context. He sees the forest when the rest of us only see trees. He has thus pushed me to think about things in ways I otherwise would not have done. This volume is another instance. Among his other intellectual and professional pursuits, Harry has become something of an expert on forecasting and political risk analysis, as a result of a year he spent as Director of Research at the Eurasia Group in

New York. As I was planning and thinking through this volume, he was extremely helpful in getting me to read into the political risk literature broadly—while this book may not reflect the paradigms of this mini-profession of risk analysis, the literature did help me to conceptualize the study. For all of these reasons, I am deeply grateful to Harry and have always held him in very high personal and professional regard—and therefore I admiringly dedicate this volume to him.

Preface

This is a relatively short book about a Big Topic: China's future. As one of the key global uncertainties over the coming decades, China's evolution will continue to have consequences—for better and for worse—for the whole world. China's future development is also going to be *the test* of longstanding debates among social scientists over whether political democratization must accompany economic modernization. To date, there has not been a single case of a country that has developed a modern economy without also democratizing. The experience of other newly industrialized economies (NIEs) is that democratization is not only a *consequence* of modernization—it is also a necessary *facilitator* of it. At a minimum, they are symbiotic processes.

China's authoritarian government has distinctly and righteously rejected this linkage, yet so far it has succeeded in facilitating the country's dramatic development. But now China has reached a qualitatively different level of development—the transition from a newly industrialized economy to a fully "mature" one—where the experiences of all other successful newly industrialized economies suggest that a more open and democratic political system is necessary in order to achieve the economic transition. Those countries that have not democratized to some extent have not successfully modernized. China has bucked this universal trend to date, but can it continue to do so by maintaining its authoritarian political system? If so, or if not, what are the consequences for China's future? Will it be successful in transitioning out of the "middle income trap" and implementing various reforms to "rebalance" the economy and move up the value chain—or will its authoritarian political system prevent it from doing so? Time will tell. I explore these core questions throughout this book.

It is a particularly uncertain time in China's development. At present the nation is at a series of critical junctures in its overall evolution, facing some stark alternatives. The choices that China's leaders make—and the actions its citizens take—will have profound consequences for the country and the entire world.

Peering into China's Future

There is no shortage of speculation about China's future. A tsunami of scholarly studies on various aspects of China's "rise" have been published over the past two decades,[1] while fund managers, corporations, political risk analysts, government intelligence agencies, and futurologists all spend countless hours (and large sums of money) trying to anticipate China's trajectory. Predictably this punditry ranges across a full spectrum of possibilities, from China becoming the superpower of the twenty-first century to its stagnation or even collapse.

Trying to predict China's future is more than difficult; it can also be professionally hazardous. The Sinological landscape is littered with China watchers' wrong predictions, as the nation has continued to surprise even the most knowledgeable and seasoned observers.[2] I am acutely conscious of this record of prognostication. While I have no crystal ball that permits me to peer into the future with any certainty, and I am aware of the potential professional pitfalls, I still believe it is incumbent on China specialists to venture into the unknown and do our best to offer informed and reasoned projections about the future, so as to inform the global public. This is our professional responsibility. We are supposedly in the best position to make informed judgments. We should strive to do so by carefully mining available data and working with multiple sources (inside and outside of China), identifying the principal variables at play in the country and their trajectories, taking a macro view but being cognizant of micro issues, anticipating discontinuities, and viewing China through a comparative lens.

China is certainly distinct, but it is not unique; it is experiencing many of the same challenges that other newly industrializing economies and societies, as well as Leninist polities, pass through. Being cognizant of China's own history is also important, as distinguishable patterns within dynastic cycles are also relevant. It is also important to have an awareness of the megatrends associated with globalization that affect all societies in the world today: technological changes, the revolution in communications, international politics, ecological systems, ideational trends, social movements. China is not immune, after all, to the exogenous global forces sweeping our planet and shaping the future of humankind. We should not get caught up in the fashionable analytical zeitgeist of the day within China-watching circles. Scholars must also be vigilant against self-censorship or intimidation from the Chinese government, or the blind acceptance of fashionable propaganda narratives (提法) and slogans (口号) used by the Chinese authorities to describe their policies. Maintaining one's independent judgment is crucial.

Finally, and perhaps most important, we should not anticipate that developments in China will be linear—straight-line projections of the present ("path dependency") or "muddling through." Sharp changes of course have occurred with some regularity throughout China's history, and the country has a proven capacity to surprise the world. One should always expect the unexpected in China.

None of us are able to peer into China's future with any precision or great clarity, but if we bear in mind these guidelines some insights may result. This book attempts to adhere to my own admonitions. It is based on four decades of China-watching and on visiting or living in the country every year since 1979, and it offers my best estimations about China's future evolution over the next decade or two. Readers will see that I eschew hard-and-fast singular predictions—that would be folly. Instead, I offer a menu of alternative pathways that China could follow. Yet I do offer my estimates of which pathways are more or less likely, and what the consequences of each may be. I welcome the inevitable disagreements from other China watchers (including Chinese officialdom), but hope to stimulate readers to better understand the contemporary complexities, and to think about a range of possible alternatives for China's future.

Washington, DC
October 11, 2015

Pathways to China's Future

China has reached a series of key turning points on its developmental path and dramatic national transformation. After more than three decades of successful reforms, the nation has reached critical junctures in its economic, social, political, environmental, technological, and intellectual development, as well as in national security, foreign affairs, and other realms of policy. Diminishing returns have set in and it has become plainly evident that the main elements of the broad reform program first launched by Deng Xiaoping in 1978 are no longer applicable or sustainable for spurring China's continued modernization over the coming decades.

Change is required. Indeed, China's own contemporary leaders have evinced their deep concerns. In 2007, former Premier Wen Jiabao bluntly described the nation's economy as characterized by the "four 'uns'": "unstable, unbalanced, uncoordinated, and unsustainable."[1] And this came from the man in charge of the national economy. Wen's successor, Premier Li Keqiang, also offered a fairly dire assessment in 2015: "China's economic growth model remains inefficient; our capacity for innovation is insufficient; overcapacity is a pronounced problem; and the foundation of agriculture is weak."[2] China's current paramount leader Xi Jinping has also lamented that "the tasks our Party faces in reform, development, and stability are more onerous than ever—and the conflicts, dangers, and challenges are more

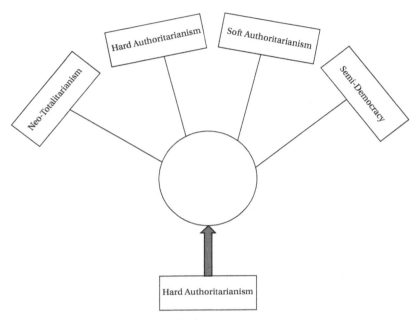

Figure 1.1 Possible Pathways for China's Future

numerous than ever."[3] So even China's leaders evince the view that the nation faces severe challenges and is at a series of turning points.

China's future is not unlike a car that approaches a roundabout, where the driver faces several roads ahead. This book argues that there are four essential choices (Figure 1.1). I label them Neo-Totalitarianism, Hard Authoritarianism, Soft Authoritarianism, and Semi-Democracy.

Like all drivers, China approaches the roundabout already on an established road. I would characterize the current path that China is on as *Hard Authoritarianism*. China's leaders, the driver of the car, have already selected this route and can continue straight ahead. This is one option, certainly the easiest option, but for the reasons explained in subsequent chapters it is not the optimal one. If they stay on this course, I judge that China will have only limited success in achieving the reforms necessary to make qualitative changes in the economy, society, and polity that will power China through its current "trapped transition" (in Minxin Pei's apt term)[4] and on to a path of sustainable development to become a mature and fully developed modern economy. Rather, if the regime stays on its current course, I predict that economic development will stagnate and even stall, exacerbating already acute social problems, and producing the protracted political decline of the ruling Chinese Communist Party.

Only by making a mid-course correction and taking a route different from that of recent years can the nation embark on decades of more dynamic growth and development—thus realizing its true potential as a superpower. Here I envision three possibilities.

At one extreme, China could lurch backward in the direction of *Neo-Totalitarianism*. This, of course, is not a positive pathway to the future. But it is a conceptual possibility that needs to be considered. Such a course correction would be stimulated by the failure of the Hard Authoritarian path to sufficiently deliver economic reforms coupled with widespread social instability across the country. Politically, the regime would be under siege. At this point a group of hardline conservative leaders would push to close China's doors to the outside and reinstitute sweeping draconian control measures inside the country. Under this scenario China would revert to a situation not unlike 1989–1992. For reasons that will be discussed in chapters 2–4, I do not see this as a feasible alternative (even if it is attempted) for three reasons. First, the private sector of the economy is already too deeply entrenched and China is too intertwined with—and dependent on—the global economy. Second, I suspect that the citizenry would resist, and perhaps revolt, if the relative freedoms they have come to know over the past forty years were rolled back. Third, I think that elements of the Party and military would not endorse such a revisionist change of national course, and these two central institutional pillars of power would therefore split. Thus, while there may well be some forces in China and in the party-state apparatus which might be tempted to recentralize state power as an answer to a stagnating economy and reform agenda (who would argue "we told you so—those reforms were not a good idea in the first place"), my judgment is that the genie is already out of the bottle and there is no going back.

A third alternative pathway would be for China to stay on the authoritarian track, but to significantly loosen its party-state controls and liberalize a variety of aspects of civic life and the political system. This *Soft Authoritarianism* alternative would, in fact, be a *return* to the course taken from 1998 through 2008. By loosening and liberalizing the way the party-state approaches the media, nongovernmental organizations, intellectuals, education, dissent, social discourse, and other aspects of civic life, the necessary conditions would be laid for qualitative changes in the economy that would better (but not completely) achieve its reform ambitions. Loosening controls on civic life would be coupled with significant changes in the way that the Chinese Communist Party operates and relates to society, thus making real political reforms within the existing one-party system. This is a far preferable course for China to take and there *is* a possibility of China altering its course on to the Soft Authoritarian track after 2017—but, for reasons elaborated in chapter 4, I judge it will likely not be the road taken.

Another potential pathway would be for China to embark on the entirely new road of *Semi-Democracy*. Democracy comes in many forms; one size does not fit all. Should China pursue this pathway it would, in all likelihood, bear a strong resemblance to the Singaporean model. In Singapore, to be sure, some rights are restricted and the ruling party remains in power. But Singapore has many aspects of democracy:

multiple political parties, regular elections, a parliament and judiciary independent of the executive, a very open media (with restrictions), real rule of law, an exemplary professional civil service, no corruption, active NGOs, a full market-driven and open economy, a multiethnic society without discrimination, a high-quality and globalized educational system, and protection of many basic freedoms and human rights. China remains a very long way from having these progressive features, and it is highly doubtful that the Chinese Communist Party would tolerate them. Nonetheless, it is not inconceivable that China could move in this alternative direction—particularly growing out of Soft Authoritarianism, if it too reached its reform limits and China remained in a "trapped transition."

Thus, these four alternative routes present themselves for China's future. As Figure 1.2 illustrates, each has its own likely consequences:

Pathway	Likely Result
Neo-Totalitarianism	Regression, Atrophy, and Collapse
Hard Authoritarianism	Limited Reform, Stagnation, and Decline
Soft Authoritarianism	Moderate Reform and Partial Transition
Semi-Democracy	Successful Reform and Full Transition

Figure 1.2 Pathways and Likely Results for China's Future

It is always easiest—for cars, people, or governments—to stay on the same course. To a large extent, nations (like cars) are "path dependent," and can only make an alteration in course by making strong decisions and allocating sustained resources to the newly chosen direction. Otherwise, the path already taken has a continuing power of its own.

In fact, it is much more difficult for nations to alter their direction than it is for cars. Even when it is evident that a chosen direction is failing, it remains difficult to alter course. Vested interests make it so. Fear of unknown consequences is another deterrent. Size is another factor. Turning a nation the size of China, even a modest degree, is more like turning an ocean liner—much less nimble than a car. It is always easiest to carry on, "muddle through," and make minor adjustments than to make fundamental alterations. The Chinese call this "crossing the river by feeling the stones" (摸着石头过河).

With these possibilities and caveats in mind, let us begin our exploratory journey through China's future by understanding the road currently taken and the choices previously made.

China Today:
Paying the Price for a Path Already Taken

Two key periods over the past decade have done much to determine the path China is on today. The first came between 2007 and 2009, when China's leaders avoided some fundamental decisions and made others. The non-decisions concerned the economy, while the proactive decisions affected the political system and society. The leadership decided to defer the tough choices for changing China's economic growth model, while at the same time deciding to cease proceeding with a package of political reforms practiced over the previous decade and to crack down. By 2012–2013 the postponed economic choices were made, however, and were coupled with the new wave of political repression.

China's real economic dilemmas became evident to many economists inside and outside of the country around 2007–2008 when it became apparent that diminishing returns from China's post-1978 economic development model had begun to take hold and a qualitatively new macro growth model was needed (as evidenced by Premier Wen Jiabao's "four 'uns'"). But Wen's warnings went largely unheeded until 2012, as the government remained path-dependent in its "comfort zone," staying with what had worked so well for three decades. Thus, the macro economic growth model of large fixed-asset investment domestically (primarily into hard infrastructure) plus low-end, low-cost export manufacturing remained intact. The situation was analogous to that of a drug addict—even knowing that the habit had to be broken, it remained easier to continue as before. Nor was there yet a clear comprehensive set of alternatives available.

The onset of the devastating Global Financial Crisis in 2008 only compounded the problem, as China's leaders looked for ways to buffer their country from the global contagion. The government's response to the crisis was "more of the same," as it unveiled a gargantuan economic stimulus package worth $586 billion (RMB 4 trillion). In hindsight, while the stimulus injected enormous new funds into the economy—thus stabilizing not only China but also stemming the global hemorrhaging—much of the money came from loosened local bank lending and "shadow banking" instruments. This only dug local governments deeper into debt and created asset bubbles. Most important, perhaps, it postponed much-needed structural reforms that would put the nation's economy on a qualitatively new and different growth path. The global financial crisis also had the ancillary effects of further convincing Chinese decision-makers that the West was in terminal decline and, concomitantly, of the efficacy of their own "China Model" (中国模式). China's foreign policy also became more "assertive" during this time.

The fiscal loosening was coupled with political tightening. While stimulus funds were flowing into the domestic economy, in an unannounced but dramatic departure beginning in 2009, the regime abruptly abandoned the political reform path it had been on over the previous decade (1998–2008). These political reforms are detailed in chapter 4. In effect, during this decade, Jiang Zemin and Hu Jintao initiated and had sought to manage political change rather than to resist it. But in 2009, for reasons described in chapter 4, the leadership reversed course, abandoned political reform, and initiated a sustained crackdown that exists to this day.

By November 2012 a new leadership had come to power at the Eighteenth Party Congress, led by Xi Jinping. By 2013 the new leadership was ready to act on the economic front in the way that the old leadership was not. Early in the year it signaled that the Third Plenum, which would convene in the autumn, would be a major and significant event, and systematic planning began for it throughout the bureaucracy. Communist Party General Secretary and President Xi Jinping took personal charge of the special leading group overseeing preparations (instead of the more likely Premier Li Keqiang). When the Third Plenum convened in November 2013 Xi, not Li, was clearly in charge. At its conclusion the plenary session issued the *Decision on Major Issues Concerning Comprehensively Deepening Reforms* and an ancillary *Explanation* of the *Decision* given by Xi Jinping.[5] The massive communiqué ran 22,000 Chinese characters in length and identified more than 300 specific reform measures in 60 separate categories.[6]

What was particularly noteworthy was the systematic and comprehensive approach reflected in the Third Plenum documents. Previously, the government had only offered piecemeal and incremental proposals for the future. The Plenum was the first serious attempt by the Chinese Communist Party and the government to grapple with the full and complex agenda of issues they confronted. The *Decision* and

Xi Jinping's subsequent *Explanation* were, at the same time, refreshingly candid in places but frustratingly vague in others. For example, it was forthright about the high number and seriousness of the problems facing the party-state, to wit:

At present, extensive and profound changes have occurred in the internal and external environments. China's development faces a series of outstanding contradictions and challenges. There are still many more difficulties and problems waiting for us in the future. For example, the lack of balance, coordination, and sustainability in development is still outstanding. The capability of scientific and technological innovation is not strong. The industrial structure is not reasonable and the development mode is still extensive. The development gap between urban and rural areas and between regions is still large, and so are income disparities. Social problems have increased markedly. There are many problems affecting people's immediate interests in education, employment, social security, healthcare, housing, the ecological environment, food and drug safety, workplace safety, public security, law enforcement, and administration of justice. Some people still lead hard lives. The problems of going through formalities, bureaucratism, hedonism, and extravagant practice are outstanding. Some sectors are prone to corruption and other misconduct, and the fight against corruption remains a serious challenge for us. The key to solving these problems lies in deepening reform.

Yet many other sections were notable for their opacity and vagueness. This suggested ongoing debates and irresolution of issues behind the scenes. Despite the lack of specificity in many aspects, the Third

Plenum *Decision* was commendable for the broad-brush sweep it took in identifying needed areas of reform. Underlying it was an acute awareness that China's old development path had run its course and a fundamentally new one was needed.

While the Third Plenum can be praised in this respect, it is note-worthy that two years later there has been so little follow-through of the *Decision*. The US-China Business Council, for example, maintains a running online tracker of its implementation—by 2015 it reported a dismal implementation rate of less than 10 percent.[7] The European Chamber of Commerce in China released a similarly downbeat assessment entitled "Third Plenum Reality Check."[8] Most other economists and China watchers are similarly unimpressed with the progress to date.

Is China Too Big to Fail?

China's reforms thus seem stuck in a trap, or series of traps. The situation today (2015) combines the hardened political repression evident since 2009 (but intensified since Xi Jinping took office in 2012) with very marginal economic reforms and increasingly acute social problems. This is precisely the new juncture China currently faces. The common denominator is the political system. To my mind, there is a *direct linkage* between politics and all other aspects of China's future.

Without a return to a path of political reform, with a substantial liberalization and loosening of many aspects of the relationship between the party-state and society, there will continue to be very marginal economic reform and social progress. This is the main argument of this book.

This is not to say that China's economy will not continue to grow if it remains on its Hard Authoritarian course, but it will do so at a much more modest and uneven pace. It will certainly continue to have some successes, but without political liberalization I assess that China will be unable to reach its growth potential and aspirations, and relative stagnation will become the "new normal." There are multiple signs that this is already the case. It will not be Japanese-style stagnation (with minimal or even negative growth coupled with deflation); it will rather be "[relative] stagnation with Chinese characteristics." A $10 trillion economy that grows at, say, 3 to 5 percent will still be significant in domestic, regional, and global terms. Such a contraction of the economy and failure to make the transition through the "Middle Income Trap" (a condition that it already finds itself in) will trigger all kinds of disruptive social and political side effects.

Thus, I see China as currently *stagnating* in what scholar Minxin Pei very astutely and presciently described in 2006 as a "trapped transition."[9] In his insightful and visionary book, Pei marshaled a sophisticated argument and considerable evidence to reveal the limits of what he describes as China's "developmental autocracy," where the economic foundation is inevitably constrained by its political super-structure. Without fundamental and far-reaching political reforms, China's economy will stagnate and the regime may well collapse, Pei has consistently argued. I did not agree with his argument at the time, but have come around to agree with him now. The reason for my changed assessment is that *China has changed in the interim*. At the time (2006) I was of the view that China was undertaking neces-sary political reforms—what I termed "adaptation" in my own book, *China's Communist Party: Atrophy and Adaptation*—that could pos-sibly alleviate the "trapped transition" Pei described. But these (Soft Authoritarian) political reforms came to a halt in 2009, and thus Pei's analysis and predictions now hold greater persuasiveness.

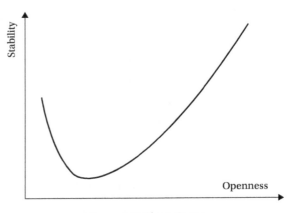

Figure 1.3 The J-Curve

A similar and insightful description of China's current dilemma is political risk strategist Ian Bremmer's concept of the "J-Curve" (Figure 1.3)—a concept that measures a nation's adaptability to change and the relationship between openness of an economy and stability of a state.[10]

Those countries that are more open—politically, economically, socially—are more stable and in a better position to revitalize themselves and withstand the inevitable pressures of globalization. Those societies that are relatively closed do not respond well to these pressures (much less unexpected shocks) and risk state failure. China, argues Bremmer, is on the left side of the J-Curve—resisting and not embracing openness. To be sure, he recognizes that China has a good deal of openness to the world; it is no North Korea. Nor is it Iran, Saudi Arabia, South Africa or Russia— all nations that he argues are sliding toward unsustainable instability. He recognizes that China has considerable openness—but it is managed and controlled openness (something of an oxymoron). Bremmer believes that China is in for significant instability as a result of its political controls, the government's secretiveness and lack of transparency, and the Party's manipulation of markets—*before* the nation can fully embrace the openness needed to ensure long-term stability and growth.

The key issue for nations like China at this stage of development is not just the economic growth model and its declining efficacy, but precisely the *relationship between economics and politics.* For economies to transition up the added-value ladder, break through the developmental ceiling, and make the kinds of qualitative transitions necessary to become truly modern and developed, political institutions must be *facilitative.* They must cease being "extractive" states and become what scholars Daron Acemoglu and James Robinson describe in their insightful book *Why Nations Fail* as "inclusive states."[11] This requires tolerance—even facilitation—of autonomous actors within society.

This line of argument is hardly new news to social scientists. Modernization theorists during the 1960s—such as Seymour Martin Lipset, Samuel Huntington, Walt W. Rostow, A. F. K. Organski, Alex Inkeles, David Apter, and others—all identified this necessity.[12] Huntington's *Political Order in Changing Societies* epitomized those who argued that authoritarian regimes were ill-equipped to facilitate a post-extractive economy and meet the rising demands of their newly wealthy citizenry.[13] Buried on page 424 of his *locus classicus* is Huntington's pithy observation, "The crucial question concerns the extent to which the system institutionalizes procedures for assimilating new groups into the system."[14] This is what Huntington meant by the third and final stage of development of authoritarian regimes—the "adaptation" phase—that follows the "transformation" and "consolidation" phases of such totalitarian/authoritarian-type mobilizational/extractive regimes. This concept of political adaptation is crucial for understanding the state of the Chinese communist regime today. Either these regimes adapt and become more inclusive, hence increasing their chances of political survival as well as facilitating socioeconomic transitions and providing enhanced public goods, or they fail to do so and ultimately die.

Modernization theorists have been joined in this conclusion by scholars of Leninist (communist)-type systems. Many scholars of "comparative communist studies" posited multistage models that all Leninist party-states essentially pass through: revolution and seizure of power → transformation and mobilization of society → consolidation of state power and extension over all aspects of society → extraction of resources and capital from society for state purposes → bureaucratization and "Brezhnevization" of state power → adaptation and limited pluralism to cope with stagnation and ossification → ? The reason there is a question mark in the final stage is because *no* communist-type political regime has yet successfully managed the institutionalization of adaptation on any kind of permanent basis.

That includes China. As is described further below and in chapter 4, the Chinese communist regime *was* attempting to adapt and become more inclusive and tolerant from 1998 to 2008—but since 2009 the party-state has recoiled and abandoned this earlier path. Even had it continued, it is uncertain that the regime could have successfully ridden the tigers of economic, social, and political reforms simultaneously. In any event, the Beijing regime has largely abandoned that path and retrenched since 2009, thus sliding back into the stage of atrophy and ossification—suppressing rather than embracing needed reforms. Zbigniew Brzezinski, in his prescient book *The Grand Failure*, published in 1989, two years before the collapse of the Soviet Union, described communist party-states in this penultimate and moribund stage as "post-communist authoritarianism." In this phase, the communist leadership loses confidence, evinces a deep insecurity, and tries to reassert control. Rule becomes rule for rule's sake. The governing rationale is stripped bare to its core: *maintaining power*. But the decay has progressed too far by this point, as the regime's traditional tools of control and mobilization begin to break down. Brzezinski recognized the hollowness and bankruptcy of such regimes in the Soviet Union and Eastern Europe, and he correctly identified this "post-communist authoritarian" phase as the precursor to the eventual implosion and collapse of communist party-states and their replacement by an entirely new phase which he identified as "post-communist pluralism."[15]

Both the modernization theorists and the comparative communism theorists have much to offer us in understanding China today and its likely future evolution. Why should China be immune to the processes that afflicted other late-stage Leninist regimes or Middle-Income-Trap newly industrializing economies—processes so amply demonstrated in decades of in-depth research in multiple cross-national studies? China is not immune to these generic phenomena. These same processes and pressures are already beginning to bite in China, and they can only be expected to intensify in the future.

This is China's current dilemma, and it is a profound one. Quite simply, it is not moving ahead politically and therefore not moving ahead economically either. China can stay on the current road—the road to continued relative economic stagnation, increased social tensions, and political decline possibly leading to the collapse of the Chinese Communist regime—*or* it can open up politically and enjoy far better chances of becoming a fully developed economy and modern country. The economic reform goals envisioned by the Third Plenum will be largely (but not entirely) unachievable unless spurred by parallel political reforms. Nor can China's many social tensions be effectively managed without a political loosening. These are the stark choices China faces.

Variables and Questions Shaping China's Future

The major determinant of China's future continues to lie with its leaders and the conscious choices they make. China remains a country that responds to cues from above. Yet China's future is only partially in the hands of the party-state. There are a considerable number of variables and exogenous factors—internal and external to the country—that are largely beyond the control of the government, yet shape its choices and the evolution of the nation. These variables and the underlying questions are discussed at length in each subsequent chapter, but allow me to identify a number of the key ones here. Domestically, one can divide these independent variables into three categories: political, economic, and social.

Politically, we must watch closely the efficacy and legitimacy of the ruling regime (Chinese Communist Party). It is not easy to see weaknesses in China's party-state, as it works around the clock to project an image of stability, coherence, strength, decisiveness, and purpose. Yet it is not as strong as it appears; the image it tries so hard to project is misleading. The Chinese have the proverb *waiying, neiruan* (外硬内软)—strong on the outside, weak on the inside. For all its strengths, I believe the CCP regime to also have multiple inherent and internal weaknesses; these are discussed in chapters 2–4. Beyond the party-state, it is important to carefully monitor the relative satisfaction or discontent among several sectors of society: youth, the middle class, intellectuals, students returned from abroad, ethnic minorities, the migrant population, and the rural population. All of these sectors have potential for political activism if their aspirations falter and frustrations reach a critical mass.

Economically, there are many variables at play. Key among them, however, is the relative scope of the state versus the private sector and market forces in the national economy. The other principal driver will be the degree to which China can become an innovative and knowledge-based economy or remain a copier and processing economy. Innovation is absolutely central to China's economic future. But it is not a simple question of being innovative or not, as China will surely become innovative in some sectors—the questions are how broadly and how deeply? A third set of economic factors has to do with the levels of debt (central, local, corporate, and bank) and asset bubbles in different sectors of the economy. China's economy is already burdened by an estimated 282 percent of total debt as a percentage of gross domestic product (GDP). This is unsustainable in the eyes of many economists, despite China's huge liquidity reserves. As for asset bubbles, 2014–2015 witnessed the bursting of urban property bubbles in several major cities, as well as the bursting of the stock market bubble on the Shanghai and Shenzhen exchanges. Excess manufacturing capacity and inventories are also problems. Another growing concern is the relative decline in foreign inbound investment, which is related to the increased costs and difficulties of operation for foreign multinationals in China. What other time bombs lurk waiting to burst in China's opaque economy?

Socially, there are multiple variables to monitor. The facilitation or repression of civil society (by the government) is one. The government's urbanization plans are another, as the scheme will involve the largest population movement in human history. Rising unrest in Tibet, Xinjiang, and across China is a major challenge. Reform or abolition of the household registration (*hukou*) system is critical to managing China's massive internal migration problem. Meeting the ever-expanding aspirations of China's burgeoning middle class will also be a central challenge, as the nation's currently estimated 300 million citizens in this category will at least double and possibly triple by

2030. As numbers of the affluent increase exponentially, already exist-ing problems of social inequality and class resentment will inevitably increase—causing polarization and increased unrest. Demographic changes will also have a huge impact on the nation's workforce and economy, as the size of the country's population aged sixty and above will increase dramatically, growing from 200 million in 2015 to over 300 million by 2030. The number of families with only one child, which is also on a continued rise, only underscores the challenge of supporting the growing numbers of elderly Chinese. Finally, corruption—which is a cancer that cuts across the society, economy, and polity—will continue to plague the nation (despite the regime's anti-corruption campaign).

China also does not evolve in a bubble: external factors remain important too. Macro trends in the world have indirect and direct effects. This includes the realities of geopolitics, including China's increasingly fraught and competitive relationship with the United States. China's ambiguous relations with its Asian neighbors will also directly affect China's own development, depending on China's own (benign or assertive) behavior in its neighborhood. China's own domestic nationalism is, of course, a factor here—driving it in a more assertive direction. The increasing geopolitical anarchy—characterized by the relative decline of American hegemony, the rise of other regional powers, and a fragmenting international institutional structure—affect all nation-states in the world, including China.[16] Global wars that might break out, with or without China's involvement, will certainly have negative consequences for China's security and development. Then there are exogenous factors largely beyond China's control: global energy supplies and prices; scientific and technological dis-coveries; new communications technologies; terrorism; transnational religious movements; climate change; or global economic shocks. The

U.S. government's National Intelligence Council's *Global Trends 2030* report identifies four "megatrends" that will likely characterize the world over the next fifteen years:[17]

- Accelerated empowerment of individuals—as a result of declining poverty rates, growing middle classes, greater educational attainment, widespread use of new communications and manufacturing technologies, and improvements in healthcare.
- Diffusion of power in international affairs—the United States will decline relative to other rising powers, there will be no global hegemon, the world will become more multipolar, and power will reside more in networks and coalitions than individual nation-states.
- Demographic patterns will shift—the whole world will experience aging populations, which will mitigate economic growth, while urbanization and migration increases worldwide.
- Demand for resources will grow markedly—the demand for food, water, and energy will grow by approximately 35, 40, and 50 percent respectively. Climate change will intensify the severity of existing weather patterns, with wet areas becoming more so and dry areas becoming more arid.

The NIC's vision of the world in 2030 further identifies six "game changers," variables or trends that are quite possible:

- A more crisis-prone global economy.
- An increased "governance gap" at global and national levels, as a result of the diffusion of global power, no hegemon or set of international institutions to enforce order, and the proliferation of transnational challenges.

- Potential for increased conflict at the intra-state and possibly inter-state levels, with transnational threats such as terrorism, cyber attacks, and lethal technologies spreading.
- Wider scope for regional instability, particularly in the Middle East and South Asia. East and Southeast Asia also have growing potential for inter-state conflict.
- New technologies appear that will boost productivity and mitigate resource depletion.
- The global role of the United States is indeterminate. Its power will decline relatively vis-à-vis other rising powers and as other regions south of the equator further develop—but it remains uncertain whether the U.S. will remain engaged or disengage from world affairs.

These and other external variables could all have an impact on China's future trajectory and they should be borne in mind as we now turn to explore China's possible futures in greater depth in chapters 2 (on the economy), 3 (on society), 4 (on the polity), and 5 (on foreign relations). In each chapter I identify how the four possible future pathways described in this chapter would affect each sphere over the next ten to twenty years.

2

China's Economy

China's economy is currently confronting both a downturn in its growth rate and a wide variety of structural adjustments. These are simultaneous and secular trends that can be expected to continue over the next decade and perhaps beyond. The questions are: how low will the GDP growth rate go until it reaches a new equilibrium, and how successful will China be in making the needed structural adjustments to facilitate another lengthy period of dynamic growth and creation of a fully developed economy? These interrelated questions will be central to understanding China's economic future. Maintaining high growth rates (of 6 percent or more) may, ironically, reflect relative *failure*—showing that China remains wedded to its old growth model and hence is not making the necessary structural adjustments to transition to the new growth model. Conversely, lower growth rates (3–5 percent) may indicate successful structural transformations and longer-term developmental stability.

While the performance of the economy will remain central to China's broader future, it is actually the relationship between economics and politics that will be the key. It is very doubtful that China will be able to successfully navigate its way through the complex thicket of needed structural adjustments in the economy without parallel political reforms. A variety of social pressures are also influencing both the economy and the political system, requiring far-reaching social reforms as well (see chapter 3). China's political system was a great facilitator of the first wave of economic reforms post-1978—spurring GDP growth twenty-six-fold over the past thirty-seven years—but now and into the future it may be the greatest single impediment to further decades of reform and growth (unless it changes). China is trying to create a modern economy with a premodern political system. China's economic future requires a very different kind of Chinese party-state than in the past—no longer an administrative, commandist, centralized, extractive, and dictatorial state. Rather, it will require a state that is more reactive, responsive, inclusive, facilitative, compromising, tolerant, transparent, and genuinely decentralized.

Without this fundamental switch in the way the Chinese party-state functions, China's economic reforms will stall and the macro economy will stagnate (relatively). This does not mean that the Chinese economy will crash, although the volatility and overall economic contraction experienced in 2015 caused some analysts to predict a hard landing. GDP growth officially fell to 7 percent during the first half of 2015, while total trade declined 6.9 percent. Some analysts believe GDP growth is actually 1 to 2 percentage points lower. In the years ahead it is not inconceivable that it may fall to 5 percent or less per annum. As noted above, this is not necessarily a bad thing, as it would indicate structural shifts in the economy away from fixed asset investment toward a more variegated growth model. Moreover, given the overall size of China, its population and macro-economic heft, even 3 to 5 percent growth in a $10–$15 trillion (it is $8.9 trillion at present) economy is nothing to sneer at, although a drop to this level would have significant international implications.

Whether expanding or contracting, as the world's second-largest national economy China will continue to have a major impact globally. China currently accounts for 16.4 percent of global GDP; it contributes about 35 percent of global growth; and it accounts for about 11 percent of global trade. China's economic footprint is now truly global, with its businesses investing and operating all over the world.[1] The scope and magnitude of China's economy thus has truly global implications. If the Chinese economy catches a cold, as it did during the summer of 2015, the virus quickly spreads internationally. It is thus vital to understand the deeper dynamics of China's economy and where it is headed.

Where Do They Want to Go?
The Third Plenum Revisited

The starting point for understanding where the Chinese economy is today and where the government intends for it to go over the next few decades is the blueprint set forth in the Third Plenum documents of November 2013. I discussed this briefly in the previous chapter, but allow me to elaborate further.

The Third Plenum planners had the benefit of being able to draw upon two previous important documents. The first was the Twelfth Five-Year Plan (2011–2015), which included the central objective of moving toward a more diversified and sustainable growth model (although it postponed major decisions).[2] The second was the *China 2030* report written jointly by the World Bank and the Development Research Center of the State Council and published in 2013.[3] This massive 500-page study was initiated by former Premier Wen Jiabao and then–World Bank president Robert Zoellick. Together they envisioned the study as a guiding blueprint for transitioning to a new macro growth and development model. The central focus of the report was the need to spur technological innovation, green development, financial reforms, more egalitarian social policies, better use of factor endowments (land, labor, capital), and deeper integration into the international economic order. Detailed proposals were offered in each of these areas.

The Third Plenum *Decision* and *Explanation* were very lengthy exposés, and (as noted in chapter 1) credit should be given to the government for responding to the need for a new comprehensive reform plan.[4] Yet, on the whole, the documents were also remarkably vague—probably indicating ongoing and unresolved debates behind the scenes. This is not to say that there are not some places where specific proposals are offered, such as: loosening of the one-child policy; abolition of the "reform through labor" system; the announcement that "markets should play the decisive role in the allocation of resources"; making government budgets more transparent; more fully funding public welfare expenditures; undertaking some financial sector reforms; granting rural farmers greater property rights; creating some new bureaucratic mechanisms such as the State Security Commission, the Leading Group on Comprehensive Deepening of Economic Reform; and hints about a super environmental agency so that there is "a single department in charge of regulating and controlling all land space usage within the country's territory and to uniformly carry out protection and restoration of the mountains, waters, forests, fields, and lakes."

While it *did* signal the need for a new comprehensive reform path, and it redefined the central government's role in managing the macro economy, the Plenum documents really did very little to signal or specify how to get there (no indication of sequencing or prioritization). This lack of specificity is likely one of the three main contributing factors to the almost complete lack of follow-through in implementation following the Plenum. Another reason is that the Party's anti-corruption campaign has paralyzed the cadre corps, who are not doing their "day jobs" by carrying out the reforms. To the extent that corruption was a facilitator of economic activity (and it was), it has also compromised implementation of reforms. The third reason is that some of the intended reforms threaten deeply vested interests—notably in state-owned enterprises, manufacturing, finance, and local governments—and are thus encountering substantial (and predictable) resistance. In August 2015, a sharply worded article in Beijing's *Guangming Daily* lamented, "The scale of resistance [to the reforms] is beyond what could be imagined."[5] As a result of these factors, much of the Third Plenum reform plan stalled before it even took off.

If there has been progress in the two years since the Plenum it has mainly been in the regulatory realm. The government has issued a raft of regulations in various areas and some notable progress has been made in some spheres.[6] The National Budget Law was amended for the first time in twenty years, ostensibly allowing for greater transparency of, and citizen input into, local government budgets. Deregulation and streamlining of a wide range of central, provincial, and local administrative regulations has been a priority, with a large number of previously needed government approvals abolished. The State Council has cancelled administrative approvals on 246 items. This is very positive as it keeps with the Third Plenum pledge to "allow the market to play the decisive factor in the economy," and also reduces opportunities for bribes and rent-seeking by officials. The National Development and Reform Commission (NDRC), which previously exercised a stranglehold over economic planning, is being downsized and perhaps even broken up. It is also a main target of the anti-corruption campaign. An explicit bank deposit insurance system has been created for the first time, and pilot programs for issuance of local bonds have been set up in ten provinces and cities. The Shanghai Free Trade Zone has been established, with others probably to follow. New initiatives to further develop inland and western regions of the country have been launched, including the unveiling of the "One Belt, One Road" project to build infrastructure across Central Asia and the Indian Ocean littoral. Experiments permitting private capital to invest in utilities and the telecom sector, as well as mixed ownership of state-owned enterprises, have been launched. Government price controls on a range of goods and services have been rescinded. Tax breaks have been extended to small and medium-sized industries to spur their development, while the corporate tax rate has been reduced to 15 percent and a value-added tax (VAT) is being experimented with in order to boost local government revenue. E-commerce is being encouraged. In the area of competition policy, an anti-monopoly law was passed. China's intellectual property regime is being strengthened (at least on paper). New (draconian) laws have been drafted or passed on national security, terrorism, cyber security, and NGOs. A variety of new environmental regulations have been issued, and a number of polluting factories in Hebei province have been closed. Plans have been drawn up for the creation of a nationwide credit system by 2020. New priority is being placed on the development of the services and tourism industries. And, finally, several new leading groups have been established under the Central Committee and State Council.

These are all important initiatives, and the government should be credited with them. Nonetheless, they are mainly piecemeal and largely experimental. Foreign observers that carefully and systematically track the implementation of the Third Plenum reforms—like the US-China Business Council, American Chamber of Commerce, and European Chamber of Commerce (both Beijing-based)—all point to relative lack of follow-through to date.

As of 2014-2015 the Chinese economy began showing multiple signs of slowing down while numerous structural impediments to growth have appeared. Let's examine some of the more significant elements.

Rebalancing

At the heart of China's economic reform aspirations lies the stated desire to "rebalance" from the old (post-1978) growth model to the new one (post-2013).[7] Both the old and new growth models are based on two key components (Figure 2.1). The "old two" drivers of development were fixed asset investment (primarily into infrastructure) plus low-wage/low-end manufacturing primarily for export (this sector benefitted from large inflows of foreign direct investment). This model was wildly successful beyond anyone's expectations over the past thirty years. The "new two" envisioned catalysts for the next thirty years are domestic consumer spending plus domestic innovation and services (both of these new drivers are evaluated separately below).

The year 2013 was a decisive one economically for China. This is when the economists and the leadership really began to understand that the stimulus-heavy strategy that had allowed China to largely avoid the global financial crisis was now threatening to trigger a

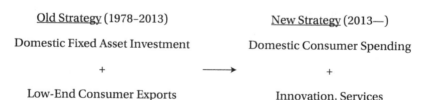

Old Strategy (1978-2013)   New Strategy (2013—)

Domestic Fixed Asset Investment   Domestic Consumer Spending

                +   ⟶   +

Low-End Consumer Exports   Innovation, Services

Figure 2.1 China's Development Strategy

domestically bred financial crisis.[8] This threat came not only from the huge increase in the stock of debt that China saw after 2008 but also in the collapsing efficiency of the credit mechanism: it takes much more credit to generate a unit of GDP now than it did five years ago. In other words, 2013 was when China's policymakers really understood the need for rebalancing—in spite of paying it lip service since 2006—because that was when it became clear that the economy needed to be weaned off its dependence on credit stimulus. It was this clear risk assessment that led to a sustained fall in credit growth and a new policy of delivering only limited, targeted, and moderate initiatives to stimulate the economy in 2014 and 2015. GDP growth inevitably fell as a result.

Actually, rebalancing is not a new objective for Chinese economic planners—it was embedded in both the Eleventh and Twelfth Five Year Plans (2006–2010 and 2011–2015)—but the fact is that after a decade of trying, they are no closer to succeeding at rebalancing. To be fair, the eruption of the global financial crisis in 2008–2009 derailed the rebalancing during the Eleventh Plan, which had the effect of perpetuating the old growth model. Under the Twelfth Plan there was a more serious attempt at rebalancing, and greater progress was made: investment growth and bank credit expansion slowed down; the share of household consumption in GDP rose; and tertiary (services) sector growth is now faster than secondary sector growth (in industry, construction, and mining). For the first time since the start of Deng's reforms, services now contribute more to GDP than manufacturing.[9] The Thirteenth Five Year Plan will take effect in 2016, and rebalancing will remain central in it.

The main reason for the need to rebalance has to do with the so-called Middle Income Trap. This is a concept used by developmental economists to describe a newly industrializing economy that reaches a mean income threshold—usually about $11,000 (China is currently at $7,593, or about $11,850 PPP equivalent, according to the World Bank)[10]—which begins to compromise the economy's competitive advantages in low-wage manufacturing. A related concept is the "Lewis Turning Point," named after the economist W. Arthur Lewis, who found that there is a point in the development process where cheap and excess rural labor is negated by wage increases as the supply of "surplus" labor is exhausted.[11] At this point in the developmental process the comparative advantage of countries like China begins to erode—thus causing a fundamental shift in the structure of the labor market (especially for low-skilled workers)—and forces them into the Middle Income Trap. Thus the "trap" (precisely what China faces now) is that the economy needs to transition up the productivity ladder by producing more knowledge-intensive goods, investing in innovation, and retraining workers from production to service and other value-added industries. In addition, to facilitate these transitions, governments must have a more modern financial system, a more open political system, and make more efficient use of factor endowments (land, labor, and capital). These are not easy transitions for China to make—and, to date, there is minimal evidence that they are occurring.

There is nothing automatic about newly industrializing economies successfully navigating their way through and out of the Middle Income Trap, although Japan, South Korea, and Taiwan did so.[12] Indeed, most do not succeed. Chinese governmental economists are painfully aware of the historical record. A comprehensive study of China's development possibilities over the next decade undertaken by the State Council's Development Research Center observed: "Around the world 101 economies joined the ranks of middle income countries after 1960. As of early 2008, only thirteen of them moved up to the higher-income club and achieved the transition successfully, including Japan, South Korea, Taiwan, Hong Kong, Puerto Rico, Mauritius, Singapore, and Israel. Most of the rest of the countries failed to finish this process and saw economic stagnation, even recession, half-way catching up but getting stuck in the Middle Income Trap. Latin American nations and the countries of the former Soviet Union and Eastern Europe are typical examples of that."[13]

The scope and scale of inhibiting factors in China's case are far greater. Finance Minister Lou Jiwei recently admitted in a speech at Tsinghua University that there was only a 50 percent chance of escaping the Middle Income Trap.[14] But, concomitantly, if China succeeds in doing so it will produce an economy the likes of which the world has never witnessed.

Growth Rates

There has been a steady decline in the national economic growth rate in recent years (Figure 2.2), but this is entirely to be expected given the diminishing returns of the post-1978 growth model. Gone forever are the days of 8, 9, or 10 percent growth.

At the National People's Congress in March 2015, the government downgraded the projected GDP growth rate for the year from 8 to 7 percent and officially declared this to be the "new normal." Some economists judge it could actually be in the range of 5–6 percent, or even lower. Even Premier Li Keqiang told the post-NPC news conference: "It will by no means be easy to meet this target." Others believe that 7–8 percent growth is attainable.

The question is not so much for 2015–2020, but for subsequent years. In this respect, I had an interesting conversation at the end of

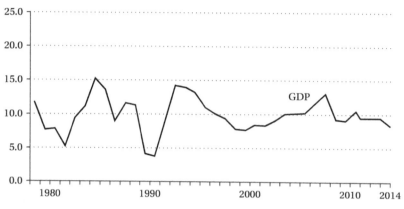

Figure 2.2 China's GDP Growth Rates

2014 with an official from the Development Research Center, the State Council's main internal think tank, who said that they had done studies projecting a progressive decline to around 3 percent by 2020–2025, and then hoped to sustain that rate for a number of years.[15] When I asked him if this was not alarming, he nonchalantly replied that it was entirely "natural," to be expected for newly industrializing economies, and even *desirable* for China! Indeed, many governments would welcome sustained 3 percent growth and we should recall, again, that an economy with the aggregate size of China's growing at 3 percent per annum remains in a league by itself.

If China's GDP growth does follow this pattern, it would be entirely commensurate with the experience of other East Asian NIEs. Economist David Dollar of The Brookings Institution has done a study of China's economy at present compared with the historical development experiences of Japan, South Korea, and Taiwan. He finds striking parallels (as well as some discontinuities) as these economies transitioned from the "takeoff" and "early stage of development" to a "mature economy." Dollar observes: "Beginning at about the stage of development where

China is now, there was a tendency for growth rates to decline [in these countries]."[16] Japan's growth rate began a precipitous decline in 1967 from a high of 11 percent growth, stabilizing around 5 percent from 1972 to 1989, and then falling to under 2 percent from 1990 to the present. South Korea and Taiwan were later developers, but followed the same pattern. Their sweet spot for high growth lasted from 1968 to 1988, then hovered between 4 and 6 percent until 2006, then declined to under 4 percent since.

We can thus expect that China will follow the same pattern. But estimates vary as to eventual equilibrium rate of GDP growth. In a report published at the end of 2013, before the volatility in the Chinese economy during 2015, Goldman Sachs estimated that it will average 5.1 percent but steadily decline to 4.1 percent by 2022.[17] Other analysts optimistically predicted China will be able to maintain 6–7 percent growth until 2020 or beyond.[18] Still others, myself included, are more pessimistic (realistic)—predicting 4–5 percent until 2020 and then likely leveling off at around 3 percent subsequently. Figure 2.3 illustrates these varying scenarios.

Worrying Sectoral Signs

There are concerning trends in certain sectors of the economy. These are each serious in their own right, but the cumulative effect on national economic health is indicative of the underlying serious structural weaknesses in the economy.

In mid-2015 China's stock market tanked, dropping 30 percent and wiping out $3.5 trillion in capitalized value over a two-week period during July. To be certain, stock markets are very different from national economies, but they are also illustrative. In response to the

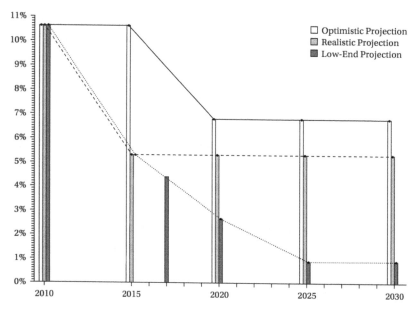

Figure 2.3 China's Alternative GDP Projections

unprecedented freefall, the government swiftly intervened by loaning $42 billion to twenty-one brokerage firms to buy stock, announced a $40 billion economic stimulus plan, ordered a halt to short selling and told half of the listed companies to stop trading of their shares, prohibited controlling shareholders and company board members from selling any shares for six months, and freezing all IPOs for six months. Altogether, the government spent at least 1 trillion yuan ($156 billion) to buy up shares in an attempt to stabilize stock prices and the market.[19] A few weeks later, China's government surprised the world and shook global markets by announcing an abrupt 4 percent depreciation in the value of its currency, the *renminbi*. On the heels of this action, on August 24, 2015, the Shanghai stock market tanked again, falling a further 7.6 percent in one day and bringing additional losses of several trillion. This "Black Monday," as it became known in China, sent global markets into further turmoil. The *Wall Street Journal* opined at the time, "China is now exporting volatility."[20] Per usual, the government intervened quickly and massively, slashing interest rates and pumping more stimulus funding into the economy.

Once again, we saw that the Visible Hand of the Chinese economy is the state. Every time the government intervenes to stem a temporary economic crisis it only exacerbates and deepens existing dependency on the state while further postponing much-needed reforms that would permit the economy to respond to real and transparent market signals.

The property market bubble has also peaked and declined precipitously in several major cities (due to oversupply and inflated prices for both residential and commercial units) while land sales are declining nationwide. The overheated market began to fall in mid-2012 and has continued a decline since, despite government intervention to prop it up. Over the subsequent two years, by mid-2014 the national property market had declined 25 percent. Beijing, Tianjin, Shanghai, and Guangzhou felt the pain first, with other second-tier inland cities experiencing big downturns in transactions and new housing starts during 2015. Northeastern cities were particularly hard hit; property investment in Heilongjiang alone plummeted 25 percent year-on-year. Among other consequences of the burst property bubble is that tax revenues (from land transactions) for local governments are declining, putting even greater pressure on their debt load and fiscal solvency. The importance of the property market cannot be understated, as it accounts for an estimated 15–20 percent of national GDP. The bursting of the bubble had long been anticipated by analysts who had tracked the blind building, overcapacity, and over-investment in the wake of the government's 2008 stimulus package. Massive "ghost cities" stand eerily empty across the country.[21] While it was a necessary self-correction, many ordinary Chinese who had bought homes for the first time are left with depleted equity; it will take a very long time to recover their initial investments. For China's middle class and ordinary first-time investors, the twin "scissors effect" of the stock market and property market bubbles bursting has hit them hard. It is made worse by the fact that many of these eager citizens borrowed from secondary "shadow banking" entities to buy stock or a flat, and are now left with crippling debt.

Chinese officials have only themselves to blame as they openly encouraged the rise in share prices in 2014 and 2015, precisely because it suited their strategy of trying to reduce the economy's dependence on credit: a buoyant stock market would give companies a way of funding themselves that did not put more debt on their balance sheets. So they miscalculated twice—by encouraging the rise in stock prices and then intervening when the market fell.[22] This raises questions about the competence and credibility of economic policy-making. A further reason for the rise in stock prices was the earlier decline in property prices: in other words, equities provided an alternative to property when the latter proved an unreliable investment vehicle. So the property market's loss was, at least in 2014, the stock market's gain.

The Financial System

China's financial system may be the Achilles' heel of the entire economy. If it can be effectively overhauled the possibilities of achieving the transformation of the entire economy will be much higher. But there are a variety of deep structural challenges in this sector that are not easily rectified.

On the surface China's financial system appears to have all the elements of modernity: banks, credit agencies, insurance companies, payments systems, equity and bond markets, etc. But banks dominate financial intermediation, providing about 60 percent of loans to the private sector, according to the Asian Development Bank. Moreover, the banking system is concentrated in the four main state banks (which provide 50 percent of loans). These enormous banks all rank among the ten largest in the world by capitalization. Thus the government maintains the dominant position in the financial system. Economists refer to this as "financial repression," a situation where the government artificially depresses deposit and lending rates and orders the state banks to increase or decrease loans in line with government planning priorities.

This variability has given rise to an enormous "shadow banking" industry where individuals or businesses can turn to get quick cash when needed.[23] One reason is because the large state banks favor state-owned enterprises and small- and medium-sized enterprises (SMEs) or individuals have had nowhere else to turn for capital.[24] These unregulated loans have had several negative effects, including contributing to corruption at the local level and ballooning debt for local businesses and individuals. But shadow banking also had positive effects, namely, giving SMEs access to credit and accelerating the de facto liberalization of financial controls (interest rates and credit quotas). The shadow banking industry in China has grown to the point where the volume of its total assets amounted to the RMB equivalent of $5.2 trillion or 51 percent of GDP.[25] At present, the government is trying to rein in the shadow banks (the term "bank" is actually a euphemism for these funding vehicles), while it is also experimenting with relaxing restrictions on deposit and lending rates by introducing a floating range for deposit rates and a market-based prime lending rate for loans.[26] After twenty years of study, an explicit deposit insurance system was also introduced in 2015, whereby the state implicitly insures all deposits and will compensate up to 500,000 RMB for losses.

But these are baby steps. The entire banking system is in need of top-to-bottom overhaul. In addition to seventeen "tier one" banks (including the four main state commercial banks: Agricultural Bank of China, Industrial and Commercial Bank of China, China Construction Bank, Bank of Communications), the country has a sprawling pyramid of other banking institutions: "joint stock" banks, state "policy banks," so-called second-tier commercial and municipal banks, urban cooperative banks, rural credit cooperatives, trust and investment corporations, micro-finance institutions, and venture capital funds. The Budget Amendment Act of 2014 was a first important step toward systemic reform, but much more needs to be done.

Essentially the government is faced with two contradictory tasks: strengthen regulation of the system (particularly shadow banking) but divest itself of excessive control of the banks, interest rates, and other areas where state intervention should give way to market mechanisms. This is a tricky and contradictory conundrum. The basic problem is what the World Bank calls the "misaligned roles of the state" in China's financial system. In its June 2015 special report on reform priorities in China's financial sector, the World Bank took China to task for a number of financial system maladies: the "structural mismatch" between local government revenues and expenditures; repressed deposit rates that lead households to the shadow banking system; "massive expansion of credit and investment"; ineffective policies to promote capital market development; ineffective financial and legal infrastructure to expand access to SMEs and households; pervasive ownership and control by the state of financial institutions (de facto ownership control of 95 percent of commercial bank assets); inability to articulate a strategic rationale for various financial institutions; distortion of banks' lending criteria.[27] The World Bank's report concluded that the Chinese government should "design and implement an exit strategy" from the financial sector.

To be successful, banking sector reform must move *in tandem* with other needed reforms: domestic capital market reform, rural land market reform, labor market (*hukou*) reform, procurement and contracting reform, compensation reform for cadres, state-owned enterprise reform, further exchange rate liberalization, convertibility and internationalization of the *renminbi*.[28] Managing such a complex financial reform package will not be easy. Even some of the more optimistic observers of China's economy are skeptical that the labyrinth of interconnected financial weaknesses can be effectively untangled and strengthened. For example, former U.S. Secretary of the Treasury Henry Paulson (who interacts extensively with China's leaders) admits in his recent book *Dealing with China*, "Frankly, it's not a question of if, but when, China's financial system, particularly the trust companies, will face a reckoning and will have to contend with a wave of credit losses and debt restructurings. . . . The issue is how big the losses will be and whether the resulting disruption in the financial market can be kept from spilling over into the broader economy."[29]

At the heart of the financial puzzle lies China's overall national debt problem (central, local, and corporate), which looms like a large thundercloud over the entire economy. So far the Chinese proverb 雷声大雨点小 (much thunder, little rain) is apt, but this is changing and rapidly. These three levels of debt now total $28.2 trillion or 282 percent of GDP.[30] Most economists believe this is not sustainable. It is also the *rate of increase* that is noteworthy: China's total debt load has *quadrupled* since 2007—the fifth fastest increase in the world. Only Greece, Ireland, Singapore, and Portugal's debt-to-GDP ratios have increased more rapidly.[31] Of these three levels local government debt is the most worrisome, although corporate debt is of rising concern. Central government liquidity is not deemed to be a problem as China sits on nearly $4 trillion in foreign exchange reserves and has no appreciable foreign debt (less than 10 percent of GDP since 2008). But local and corporate debts are ballooning. Local government debt is now estimated to be 17.9 trillion RMB or $2.4 trillion.[32] Much of the local government debt, as well as shadow banking debt, is in unrecoverable nonperforming loans (NPLs)—which will eventually have to be written off or absorbed by another round of injected funds from the Center.[33] Shadow banking debt is now estimated at $8 trillion.[34] Most analysts believe that the corporate debt problem is a much bigger problem than local government debt, as ultimately the central government could absorb local government liabilities. On aggregate, corporate debt accounts for approximately two-thirds of China's entire debt burden (approximately $19.8 trillion). So far, though, little has been systematically done to deal with the looming crisis (aside from some local bond issuance initiatives) and there are genuine worries that this is the next—and most severe—bubble to burst in the Chinese economy.

Underlying the debt problem is the over-investment problem. China's economic model for the last three decades has rested on ever-expanding domestic investment that, in turn, is dependent on ever-expanding credit. Whether through the main state banks or the shadow banking industry, China's government has consistently primed the pump. And it has done so in large part because the Party's own legitimacy is dependent on constant growth. This is not sustainable in the long term, or even in the medium run. As Nobel Prize–winning economist and commentator Paul Krugman pointedly put it: "China's leaders appear to be terrified—probably for political reasons—by the prospect of even a brief recession. So they've been pumping up demand by, in effect, force-feeding the system with credit, including fostering a stock market boom. Such measures can work for awhile, and all might have been well if the big reforms were moving fast enough. But they aren't, and the result is a bubble that wants to burst."[35]

Personal Consumption and Spending

Increasing consumer spending is a centerpiece of the government's plan to shift the overall macroeconomic growth model from the "old two" drivers to the "new two" elements. While the data on increased total consumption spending has been very positive over the past several years (averaging between 50 and 55 percent of GDP growth from 2011 to 2014), lowered GDP growth will definitely have an impact on disposable income (which only grew at single digits in 2014 after double-digit growth the previous decade). Some analysts foresee consumption expenditures slowing considerably as consumer confidence dips—especially for young professionals—while others point to the huge pent-up savings that could be unleashed.[36] Government procurement, which is also counted as part of total consumption spending, may also contract. Even if it slows overall, consumption spending is now a main driver of economic growth. China has the world's highest household savings rate of 51 percent, which, if spent, could power the economy indefinitely.

Yet the potential remains unrealized because Chinese consumers hedge against uncertainties of the future. The main uncertainty remains the necessity of saving for medical emergencies and retirement, which is the main factor accounting for China's extraordinarily high household savings rate. Another factor is the limited options for investing. Because of capital controls Chinese citizens are severely limited from investing abroad or moving their savings to foreign banks, and the government rightly fears that if these controls were further relaxed the result would be massive capital out-flight. Money moved abroad is not money spent at home. Despite the nonconvertibility of the *renminbi* on capital account and government regulations on moving money out of the country, private Chinese capital is increasingly flowing overseas. The global real estate market—from Europe to North America to Southeast Asia to South America and Africa—has boomed as a result of Chinese purchases of property. It is not just individuals investing abroad; Chinese corporations and government entities are also doing so.[37] China's non-financial outbound direct investment (ODI) totaled $121 billion in 2014, while President Xi Jinping has declared that China will invest a whopping $1.25 trillion worldwide by 2025.

Despite the exodus of capital and the government's relaxation of capital controls on a phased basis,[38] Chinese consumers still have enormous potential to drive the next wave of economic growth if their anxieties about retirement, healthcare, and old age provision can be ameliorated. People's Bank of China Governor Zhou Xiaochuan also signaled to the International Monetary Fund recently that China planned the "managed convertibility" of its currency in a step-by-step manner.[39] On November 30, 2015 China succeeded in having the *renminbi* included in the IMF's basket of currencies that enjoy "special drawing rights" (SDRs).

State-Owned Enterprise Reform

Another huge challenge is undertaking state-owned enterprise (SOE) reform—but, like other areas, it too is a huge conundrum.[40] Unlike the SOE problem twenty years ago when the rust-belt factories in the northeast and eastern seaboard cities were bleeding the national economy by running deeply in the red while not turning profits or producing goods that were competitive in the marketplace, today the challenge is making them more competitive and less monopolistic. Reducing the monopolies that SOEs hold over various key sectors of the economy—energy and raw materials, power generation, transportation (air, rail, shipping), telecommunications, aerospace, defense industries—is not going to be easy given the interlocking ties that these behemoths have to the party-state (their senior management is controlled by the Communist Party's Organization Department). China's SOEs are the epitome of deeply vested interests, with no small degree of cozy corruption deeply embedded within them.[41] The symbiotic relationship between SOEs and state banks is a form of protectionism that will be very difficult to break, as SOEs absorb over 60 percent of corporate loans from the four big state banks and 90 percent of bonds issued.[42]

Indeed, it is not entirely clear that the government and Third Plenum reform program seeks to break them up—to the contrary, the Third Plenum documents indicate that the government seeks greater efficiency and profitability from the SOEs. China has long been enamored with the South Korean *chaebol* and Japanese corporate conglomerate models of large-scale horizontally integrated firms. Indeed, the Third Plenum specifically declared that "state ownership is a central pillar of the economy," while at the same time claiming that "markets should play a decisive role." While there have been some experimental moves since the Plenum to introduce more diversified "mixed ownership" (state-private) and to publicly list parts of the SOEs in some pilot experiments, overall not much reform is taking place in this sector. A special directive from the General Office of the

CCP Central Committee issued in August 2015 specifically rejected widespread privatization and explicitly stated, "The Party's leadership of state-owned enterprises must be upheld."[43] It is thus more likely that the Party leadership does not intend to weaken—but rather strengthen—these SOEs. If this is the case, unless and until these monopolies are broken up, China will not witness much innovation or economies of scale in these sectors.

Nicholas Lardy's *Markets Over Mao*, an exhaustive study of private sector versus state sector business in China, shows clearly that innovation and growth is coming from the former and not the latter sector.[44] Lardy, a leading American economist on China, argues that the SOEs continue to be a big drag on the overall economy. Of the total 280,000 SOEs nationally, 115 are managed by the State-Owned Assets Supervision and Administration Commission (SASAC), an organ created in 2003 and charged with turning these "strategic emerging industries" into "national champions." They have combined assets of $10.5 trillion.[45] They may be significant in terms of revenue, as several populate the Global Fortune 500 list, but precious few are globally competitive. While many analysts perceived China's state sector and SOEs to be rebounding and gaining market share and corporate clout during the early 2000s (国进民退), Lardy sharply dismisses this argument. "One of the best-kept secrets about most of China's biggest SOEs is their poor performance," Lardy observes.[46] Growth and innovation, he argues, are coming from the 6.5 million private enterprises and 40.6 million household businesses across China—which accounted for between two-thirds and three-quarters of GDP between 2010 and 2012. They are already innovating new business models (particularly in e-commerce). Let us now look more carefully at the question and role of innovation in China.

The Key to Success: Innovation

Innovation is the key test for China if it is to accomplish the overall macro-economic transition and become a fully modern society and economy. This is crucial if China is to avoid becoming stuck forever in the Middle Income Trap. The only way out of the trap (as Japan, South Korea, Taiwan, and other newly industrialized economies have demonstrated) is through innovation, which enables moving up the productivity and economic value chains.

Becoming an innovative society and knowledge economy is the principal task facing the nation, and it is cited as such in all major government documents and leaders' speeches. Yet, China's economy today remains an assembly and processing economy, not a creative and inventive one. Moreover, most of the goods that are assembled or produced in China for export are intellectually created elsewhere. China's rampant theft of intellectual property and its government programs to spur "indigenous innovation" (which pour billions into domestic R&D every year) are clear admissions of its failure to create. This may, and likely will, change over time, but to date China is not setting global standards in hardly any technologies or product lines (or in the natural sciences, medical sciences, social sciences, or humanities). Chinese do not win Nobel prizes for their research, and mainland Chinese universities other than Tsinghua, Fudan, and Peking University (which currently rank among the top 100 in the *Times Higher Education Global Rankings*) are also not globally competitive. At present China does not rank very high on global indices for innovation. On the Bloomberg Innovation Index ranking of most innovative countries in 2015, China ranked No. 22 overall.[47] Nor does China rank in the top ten of the World Economic Forum's innovation rankings.[48]

Recognizing this overall shortfall, it is also true that some Chinese companies are becoming very innovative and producing cutting-edge technologies in biotechnology, nanotechnology, consumer electronics and hand-held devices, medical instruments, telecommunications equipment and software, robotics, green energy technologies and energy-saving vehicles. China's space program, high-speed rail, and deep-sea manned submersibles have all captured international attention. As President Xi Jinping himself has noted, "China has entered the advanced ranks of the world in some important fields. In certain fields, it has become a 'forerunner' or 'parallel runner' instead of a 'follower.'"[49]

Most of these breakthroughs are the result of government prioritization and R&D investment—but a growing share is coming from the corporate sector. The government has identified ten priority "strategic industries" as part of the "Made in China 2025" program: new IT technologies, numerical control tools and robotics, aerospace equipment, ocean engineering equipment and high-tech ships, railway equipment, energy-saving and new-energy vehicles, power generation equipment, new materials, biological medicine and medical devices, and agricultural machinery. China has real ambitions to become the global leader in these high-end manufacturing sectors by 2025.[50] It is already the world's largest producer of 220 kinds of industrial goods, and China overtook the United States in 2006 to be the largest exporter of high-tech products in the world (garnering 17 percent of global market share).[51] Yet, Chinese companies eye even greater potential.

China will certainly innovate over time—that is not the question. The questions are *how much, in which fields,* and *what are the impediments/facilitators* of broad-gauged long-term innovation (and can they be overcome)? Here I am more skeptical. So are others.[52]

The Chinese government seems to believe that all that is needed to spur innovation is to invest in it—like building high-speed rail or other infrastructure. China's government is indeed putting increasingly large sums into research and development (R&D), now 2.1 percent of GDP. While rising, China's R&D spending still lags behind when compared with 2.9 percent in the United States, 2.8 percent in Germany, 3.3 percent in Japan, 3.1 percent in Taiwan, and South Korea's world-leading level of 4.2 percent of GDP. At the current rate of accelerating growth in the state R&D budget (up from 1.6 to 2.1 percent since 2012), China could overtake the United States around 2022, when it will spend more than $600 billion annually. China has a huge R&D network in terms of personnel and institutions.[53] The government has a sprawling bureaucracy of national laboratories under most of the State Council ministries and within the nation's large military-industrial complex. For decades China's military industries were chronically incapable of innovation (imitation even gave them severe problems), but that is changing rapidly. As the work of expert Tai Ming Cheung has demonstrated, China's civil-military integration and defense technological innovation is really taking off.[54]

However, innovation requires much more than government investment in R&D—it fundamentally requires an educational system premised on critical thinking and freedom of exploration. This, in turn, requires a political system that is relatively open and does not permit censorship or "no go zones" in research. Students and intellectuals must be incentivized and rewarded—not persecuted or penalized—for challenging conventional wisdom and making mistakes. The deeply ingrained rote memorization and repetitive pedagogy in Chinese education is a real impediment to creativity. The Chinese university system needs to inculcate critical thinking and open-ended exploration. Even the government's attempts to lure back Chinese researchers trained and still resident abroad (like the "Thousand Talents" program) will not be enough to offset the chronic intrinsic weaknesses of the Chinese university system (see chapter 3). These returned "sea turtles" (海归派) are provided with housing, high salaries, laboratories, research assistants, and other perks—but some complain that the conditions still do not match what they left behind in the West.[55]

Educational reform will not, in and of itself, be sufficient. China's media needs to be open, uncensored, and thoroughly connected to the world. Chinese society is not going to be able to learn from and participate in global innovation if the government authorities continue to block the internet, foreign search engines, and most international media. Until the higher education and media sectors are liberalized, China will be forever caught in the Middle Income Trap—assembling and producing but not creating and inventing.

Innovation should be thought of as a top-down, bottom-up, and outside-in phenomenon. China has the first, a little bit of the second, but is severely constricting itself from the third. The government is investing top-down in research and development (as all industrial economies do), there is a little bit of bottom-up innovation coming from small and medium-sized industries (SMEs), but there are severe limits placed on electronic connectivity between China's intelligentsia and full electronic connectivity of China's citizens with the world. This does *not* mean that China will fail in its attempts at innovation. Indeed, it will succeed (and is doing so) in many areas as a result of top-down investment and prioritization. But this is classic industrial policy, where favored industries are subsidized and protected. Innovation can—and does—occur this way. And major breakthroughs can be made. This has occurred in a variety of political systems, authoritarian and democratic alike. Top-down government investment *does* produce returns. But this single element is insufficient to create an innovative society broadly. It is one thing to incubate innovation in highly protected sectors and environments—but quite another for society writ large to serve as a wellspring for creativity. The latter requires an educational system that prizes and incentivizes critical and creative thinking, an economy that encourages small and medium-sized businesses to create new product lines, and—above all—a society that encourages individualism.

China is certainly entrepreneurial, no doubt about it. Entrepreneurship is in Chinese DNA. This was one of three major drivers of the last thirty years of dynamic growth (foreign direct investment and industrial policy being the other two). But entrepreneurship and innovation are not necessarily the same things. The latter invents new things, the former figures out (sometimes new) ways of marketing existing things. China has also had a long tradition of imitation—from imperial landscape painting to modern consumer goods—as well as making incremental improvements on existing products and technologies (sometimes stolen or pirated). These traditions may be considered innovative but they are not really inventive. If and when Chinese create and invent, intellectual property rights need to be protected.

China has also had a longstanding penchant to invest in applied rather than basic scientific research—owing to a predilection for immediate solutions rather than indeterminate open-ended basic research that has an intellectual question but not necessarily an end-product in mind. This will be a limiting factor on within-firm R&D (which is growing). China is also beginning to outsource R&D abroad, in an effort to tap the advantages of foreign research environments. According to data from China's Ministry of Commerce, about 100 industrial parks and R&D centers have been established abroad.[56] This trend, to my mind, is another indication of the impediments China's potential creators face domestically—very similar to students going abroad *en masse* for their educations.

Finally, in today's globalized and interconnected world it is absolutely imperative that professionals and individuals be thoroughly networked 24/7 with their counterparts around the world. Creativity is very much a cross-border and transnational enterprise. China definitely lacks this feature because of the government's strict controls on information, travel, and even interaction with foreigners inside China.

China is definitely going to be the major test case in human history of whether political liberalization is necessary for broad-based innovation in a society. Some observers are very bullish about China's chances to become an innovative superpower.[57] For its part, the Chinese government and corporate chiefs are also doing their best to try and sell their country's innovation potential. I may be proven wrong, but I argue that China's capacity for innovation will be severely limited by its lack of political liberalization (even within its one-party authoritarian system). There has never been a single case of a country having an innovative economy absent democracy or soft authoritarianism. But, again, to be clear: it is not a question of innovation vs. no innovation. It is a question of the *scope* of innovation. China *will innovate* and produce world-class technologies and products regardless of its political system. It is rather a question of how much and how broadly will it innovate? If it practices Soft Authoritarianism—like Singapore or former South Korea—rather than the Hard Authoritarianism of today, China's chances of successful innovation will be much higher. If China fully democratized with completely open media, freedom for its intellectuals and citizens, and full connectivity with the world—then it would become an innovative powerhouse. Until then, its successes will likely be limited.

Pathways to China's Economic Future

The above analysis illustrates my belief that China's economy at present is precisely at the roundabout in the road I described in chapter

1: reforms have bogged down (actually they have never really taken off since the Third Plenum) and the economy is stagnating relative to its previous growth. This leads me to conclude there are four possible paths for the Chinese economy over the next decade.

Hard Authoritarianism, Limited Reform, and Relative Stagnation

The first scenario is a continuation of the current situation of Hard (political) Authoritarianism and relative (economic) stagnation. Minxin Pei aptly describes this as a "trapped transition."[58] Under this scenario, China's economy would continue to grow on the order of 3–5 percent per year, some of the reforms of the Third Plenum package would be implemented, but the vast majority would not. Numerous structural imbalances and chronic maladies (such as debt) would continue to plague the economy, the need to maintain growth and employment would necessitate a continuation of fixed-asset investment from the old development model, innovation would only be partially successful (thus not permitting China to fundamentally change its export composition), and the vested interests in the state sector would reassert themselves and thus compromise the transition to a more market-driven economy. Relative stagnation would prevail, the economy would fail to successfully transition from the old to the new growth model, and growth rates may even remain moderately high due to high levels of state investment and easy credit (although they would more likely fall along with stagnant growth). In this scenario China would resemble the vast majority of developing economies that become stuck in the Middle Income Trap.

This is not to say that staying stuck in the current (relative) stagnation is not a viable pathway for the future. Indeed it can be. Remember that path dependency is the easiest form of "muddling through." While this course is feasible, my guess is that the stagnation would become cancerous and metastasize, causing further deterioration—leading to protracted decay over time. The economy would not be able to remain in the animated state of a trapped transition and would slip decidedly backwards and downwards. Growth could decline to 1–2 percent per annum and all the extant problems described above would compound and worsen. Third Plenum reforms would *de facto* be abandoned. This scenario would be Japanese-style stagnation with Chinese characteristics. Some analysts refer to this as the "hard landing" scenario.[59] I consider it the progressive decay scenario.[60] Such a scenario would severely test the Party's performance-based legitimacy and, taken together with other maladies afflicting the party-state (see chapters 3 and 4), could ultimately bring down the Chinese communist regime.

Neo-Totalitarianism

Under this second scenario government and Party leaders decide that the more marketized reforms are not working or are not desirable and they opt instead to take an entirely different path of *greater centralization and control*. Essentially, this alternative scenario would be centered on *strengthening the state and state sector* across the board and in all aspects of the lives of the nation. No reforms, as envisioned in the Third Plenum documents, would be enacted. This would be music to the ears of SOEs, the disenfranchised who have been marginalized over the past three decades, as well as left-leaning leaders who wish to restore a greater socialist element to China. Politically, it would involve an even greater tightening and crackdown—Hard Authoritarianism morphing into restored totalitarianism. Coercion and control (already reinforced) would be stepped up. Social and ideological conformity would be enforced by a pervasive state security apparatus. In terms of the economy, privatization would give way to renationalization and collectivization by the state. The military-industrial complex would become the favored economic sector. Strict controls would be placed on the labor market. Nationalism would spike, with possible aggressive moves against Japan and other neighbors.

While this possibility is not unimaginable, I judge it unfeasible given the already tremendous growth and dominance of the private sector of the economy and the relative freedoms that Chinese citizens do enjoy. Totalitarian economies are also not efficient. It is hard to imagine a return to the post-Tiananmen retrenchment of 1989–1992, much less totalitarian Maoist China, but it is not impossible. Xi Jinping holds and wields power today as no despotic leader since Mao has done, and there are already elements of his rule that are trending in this direction. But my sense is that such a throwback to the past would fail.

Soft Authoritarianism and Partial Reform

Under the third scenario, China takes another fork in the road. Instead of the path-dependent Hard Authoritarianism leading to relative stagnation and protracted decay, the CCP decides to return to the Soft Authoritarian model and thus breaks through and is successful in implementing many of the Third Plenum reforms . . . but not all of them. A more open polity would do much to stimulate innovation, improve governance, alleviate tensions in society, and embrace fuller marketization and greater competition in the economy. A wide variety of bottlenecks caused by Hard Authoritarianism would be neutralized or removed, as openness breeds productivity. It also breeds greater stability, as the J-Curve predicts. A return to Soft Authoritarian and more liberal approaches to politics and state-society relations would have many positive effects on the economy. But ultimately, it would not be sufficient to fully escape the Middle Income Trap and become a fully mature modern economy. That requires fuller democratization. It could also be that Soft Authoritarianism is the midwife to Scenario 4.

Semi-Democracy and Successful Reform

If China were to embrace a transition to a Singapore-style democracy, it would permit all of the qualitative changes needed to transition from the old to the new growth and development model. Under this scenario, China escapes the Middle Income Trap (by innovating its way out), resolves its debt overhang problem and fixes its financial system, introduces greater competition and market forces throughout the economy, succeeds in the government's urbanization scheme (see next chapter) and resolves the *hukou* dilemma, expands the service sector and household consumption, tackles corruption, cleans up the environment, fully taps factor endowments (land, labor, capital), becomes an innovative society, and achieves many other goals envisioned in the Third Plenum documents and the World Bank/State Council *China 2030* report. This is more than a soft landing scenario— it is the successful reform scenario.

Prospects

Economic success is not attainable absent significant political loosening and liberalization. Simply put, so many of the aspirational reforms require an across-the-board loosening of controls by the state on society. This is particularly the case concerning innovation, but also with reforming the financial system. Without greater, more comprehensive economic, commercial, and political transparency, the proclaimed market-driven reforms will be stillborn and hidden factors will continue to distort the normal functioning of the economy.

In other words, the key to China's economic future runs directly through politics. The ruling regime must make the fundamental decision to devolve power and substantially lessen the role of the party-state in the life of the nation. If the Party leadership decides to do this, embracing either Scenario 3 or 4, they will in all likelihood achieve some degree of success in their reforms, enhance their chances of staying in power, and launch China onto another three-decade wave of growth and development. If they do not, then the economy will progressively stagnate, frictions will germinate throughout society, and the regime will progressively atrophy.

Will the CCP leadership make this tough choice and decide that their collective survival, and the nation's overall future, is better served through loosening up rather than tightening up? We discuss this dilemma further in chapter 4, but my analytical instincts tell me "no." The Party leadership is too insecure to take the necessary decisions to give up the relative degree of power necessary in order to stay in power by means other than control and coercion. Therefore, the regime and system will be in a progressive state of atrophy, decay, and decline over time.

3

China's Society

No dimension of China has changed as rapidly or as thoroughly during the reform era as has society, and no society in history has experienced such profound transformations in such an abbreviated period: from an agrarian, pre-industrial, poor, uneducated, closed, conformist, and sedentary society entirely dependent on the state for basic provisions to an urbanized, industrial, increasingly wealthy, educated, open, variegated, and mobile society able to purchase most of life's necessities in the marketplace.

Anyone who has been traveling through China annually over the past (almost) four decades, as I have, can testify to the extraordinary transformations in the lives of one-fifth of humanity. I recall when I first visited in the late 1970s, the reforms were getting under way, Deng Xiaoping invoked the notion "to get rich is glorious," and Chinese urbanites aspired to possess the "four rounds" (things that went around: a bicycle, a wristwatch, a sewing machine, a washing machine) and "three electrics" (a television, refrigerator, and private telephone). Nowadays Chinese *nouveaux riches* travel and buy property abroad (in 2014 Chinese tourists took 109 million trips abroad), pay exorbitant foreign tuition prices for their children's education, own their own luxury cars, live in privately purchased homes, and have huge disposable incomes. China now has the largest number of millionaires (1.09 million) and the second-largest number of billionaires (152 plus 45 in Hong Kong) in the world.[1]

Certainly the wealth and material life of Chinese society has improved enormously. So have various quality-of-life indicators, such as per capita income ($7,593), life expectancy (75 years), literacy rate (95.1 percent), infant mortality (11 per 1000 births), fertility rate (1.7), women employed as a percentage of total professionals (38.1), percentage of population below the poverty line (6.1), percentage of secondary school enrollment (92), percentage of the population with access to health insurance and primary healthcare (95), and percentage of the population with access to telecommunications (94.5).[2] Overall, China ranks No. 91 out of 195 nations on the UN Development Indicators Index.[3] In many areas China has made enormous social progress.

But with growing affluence and improved quality of life have come a variety of serious problems and collateral challenges for China's future. Underlying them all is the unavoidable revolution that all modernizing societies face: *the revolution of rising expectations*. All strata of Chinese society have improved their lot over the past three decades, but this initiates a treadmill of never being fully satisfied, being oftentimes frustrated, and seeking perpetual improvement. The greater the social progress, the greater the expectations. Inevitably, also, there are many whose lives have not improved as rapidly or as much as others in society—thus causing widening class differentiation and jealousy. Moreover, as people get wealthier and their basic consumer needs are satisfied, they become more expectant and demanding that their governments provide better "public goods": physical safety and freedom from crime, quality education, a clean environment, better transportation, universal healthcare, national security, and so on. This is the inevitable but predictable revolution for all newly industrializing societies. For governments like China's, where popular support and regime longevity primarily depend upon what is known in political science as "performance legitimacy," the pressure to deliver an ever-improving standard of living and public goods is inexorable.

This chapter catalogues many of the major societal challenges in China today. Effectively addressing these challenges will create ongoing tasks for the government into the future. Some—such as urbanization, healthcare, education, pensions, and environmental cleanup—are occurring as a *result* of government initiatives. Others, such as social stratification or demographic transition, are occurring largely *irrespective* of government policies. And some—such as repression of the public sphere and unrest along China's periphery—are occurring *because* of government policies. In some spheres a stronger and more proactive state is required (environmental protection, public good provision), while in other domains a looser and less repressive state is needed (public sphere, Xinjiang and Tibet) in order to cope with the challenges. Let us now look more carefully at these future challenges.

China's Shifting Class Composition

Class has always been a sensitive subject in communist China. Mao's revolution was, of course, premised in large part on a socialist vision of overturning China's existing "unequal" class structure and ultimately abolishing classes altogether (except the "working class," which was supposed to be the linchpin of the "dictatorship of the proletariat," consistent with the Marxian vision). In their attempt to abolish classes, Mao and the Communist Party, in fact, actually developed *more* classes.[4] In 1950, after coming to power, the communists categorized everyone in the population into one of thirty-eight class categories (mainly defined by occupation).[5] Thereafter, the remainder of the Maoist era was dominated by class labeling, class leveling, and class warfare—culminating in the Great Proletarian Cultural Revolution (1966–1976).

The post-Mao period brought about great social diversification and stratification, as all kinds of new occupations were created in the "socialist-market economy," labor mobility took off with the loosening of the *hukou* system, and many pursued Deng Xiaoping's admonition, "to get rich is glorious!" Between 1978 and 2006 the percentage of the workforce engaged in agriculture dropped from 67.4 percent to 40.3 percent, while those engaged in private business (private entrepreneurs, private business owners and their employees) grew from 2.2 percent to 20.9 percent.[6] Rural and urban household incomes have both increased year-on-year (approximately 7 percent for rural and 10 percent for urban per annum).[7] On one end of the scale, more than 200 million people have been lifted out of poverty, an impressive achievement unmatched in history. Yet 82 million people still live below the poverty line on less than $1 per day. At the other end of the scale, as noted at the outset of this chapter, China now boasts over one million millionaires and nearly 200 billionaires. This "upper class" (高层阶级) now accounts for 6 percent of the population.[8] China's super-rich are an eclectic lot: the *Hurun China Rich List* of the 1,000 wealthiest Chinese reports their average age is fifty-one, they are fairly well educated, include 15 percent women, have made their fortunes in a variety of fields (primarily real estate and manufacturing), and live all along China's coastal seaboard.[9]

More significant has been the growth of the middle class (中层阶级) in China, which reportedly now accounts for approximately 28 percent of the population (combining upper- and lower-middle-class households).[10] This sector is anticipated to grow dramatically over the next decade. A major study by the private consulting firm McKinsey & Company projects that the upper middle class will swell to 54 percent of the urban population by 2022, while the lower middle class will shrink to 14 percent and the upper class will grow to 9 percent.[11] The major import of these findings, McKinsey argues, will be the enormous unleashing of consumer spending (they anticipate a 42 percent surge in spending by the affluent and upper middle class by 2022). The McKinsey report also interestingly predicts that the geographic concentration of the middle class will shift from the coastal to interior provinces—coastal China currently accounts for 87 percent but is expected to drop to 61 percent while inland China will grow to 39 percent of the middle class population. Consumer preferences will also shift accordingly as next-generation youth (currently in their teens and early twenties) are predicted to be much more experimental and diversified in their purchasing habits. Another study by the Asian Development Bank is even more bullish about China's middle class potential, arguing that by 2030 it will account for 80 percent of the total population.[12] This magnitude and rapidity of growth is probably unlikely, but it still points toward the dramatic social transformation that lies ahead in China.

A particularly acute social problem in China, now and into the future, is *inequality*. China is now among the top ten countries of the world's highest Gini Coefficient rankings, the main measure of social inequality in societies worldwide, although the official estimates are not in agreement. The World Bank's most recent estimate was .37 in 2011, and is the lowest, while the Chinese government's own calculation (Figure 3.1) puts it higher, at .47 for the same year, while others put it in between at .42.[13] While high, China's Gini ranking peaked around 2009 and has fallen since (paralleling a global pattern).

While not as high and acute as South Africa, Brazil, or Nigeria, China's Gini rating ranks it fourth in the world (Figure 3.2).

Inequality is not simply a statistical measure of income. As scholars

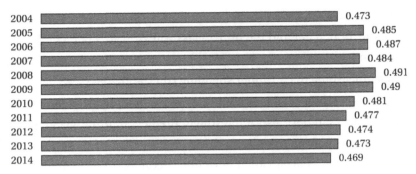

Figure 3.1 China's Gini Coefficient
Source: China National Bureau of Statistics.

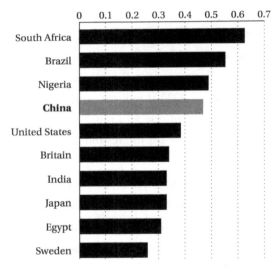

Figure 3.2 China's Gini Coefficient in Comparison
Sources: China National Bureau of Statistics; OECD; World Bank.

Jane Duckett and Guohui Wang point out, inequality involves access by individuals and households to public services such as housing, health-care, and education; it biases people in their search for employment, and it involves discrimination and unequal opportunities for women and minorities.[14]

As the work of sociologist Martin King Whyte of Harvard illustrates, inequality is also profoundly *perceptual*—how people perceive themselves and their social status and opportunities in relation to others. Do they perceive injustice and discrimination? Whyte's extensive survey research leads him to this counterintuitive conclusion: "We find little evidence of the claimed high and rising levels of popular anger about inequality issues, and we see few signs that China is heading towards a 'social volcano' due to widespread discontent over inequality and distributive injustice issues."[15] While I respect Professor Whyte enormously and I recognize the importance of his empirical data, I am very skeptical about his conclusions. In my view, Chinese society is a social tinderbox waiting to ignite—although a social volcano is not an apt metaphor; a better one is a very dry forest or grassland in summer where multiple fires can break out at any time and then spread quickly. As Chairman Mao famously professed, "A single spark can start a prairie fire." China already experiences nearly 200,000 dispersed "incidents of mass unrest" every year (Figure 3.3). My personal observations and conversations throughout China in recent years lead me to a conclusion opposite to that of Whyte. Granted, my sense is not based on large-N, multi-year and multi-local surveys; it is based on old-fashioned observations and conversations. I sense a high degree of widespread frustration across social classes and over a variety of social issues. Members of every sector of society with whom I spoke across eleven provinces during a year of living in China (2009–2010) evinced relative frustration: intellectuals, workers, farmers, youth, young professionals, minorities, migrants, some businessmen, even Party members and officials. While the incomes and opportunities for these groups have all improved substantially over time, it is a question—at noted at the outset of the chapter—of the *revolution of rising expectations*. With the slowdown in the economy, which (we

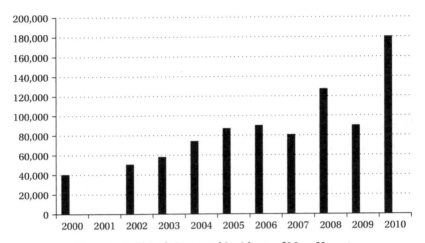

Figure 3.3 China's Reported Incidents of Mass Unrest
Sources: *Financial Times* and China Labor Bulletin.

noted in the previous chapter) is likely to continue and even deepen over the coming decade, people's opportunities will also (relatively) shrink. This will hit the middle class in particular—who constitute a potent political force. Thus, I foresee both the perceptions and the realities of social inequality growing over time.

The Communist Party and government are certainly aware of the problem—socially and economically, but also politically. This is, after all, a party-state supposedly dedicated to equality. And China's society, somewhat similarly to that of Europe, expects the government to proactively address the problem of inequality. For its part, the government has used a variety of policies and instruments aimed at narrowing the growing wealth gap: taxes, transfer payments, grain price supports, tuition waivers for rural youth attending school, subsidized urban housing and healthcare, poverty alleviation, direct investment for developing the interior and western parts of the country, and other schemes. These are all commendable programs. Time will tell, though, if they will be enough to address the increasingly severe problem of social stratification in China. I have my doubts.

One clear indicator of the social instability that grips China is the escalating number of "incidents of mass unrest" that occur each year. According to Ministry of Public Security statistics, these incidents (defined as events with 100 or more participants) have increased steadily over time, from 8,700 in 1993 to 120,000 in 2008.[16] Some reports put the total as high as 180,000–210,000 in 2013–2014 (see Figure 3.3).

Some incidents have been very large-scale, ranging from several hundred participants to 10,000 or more. The vast majority of these protests are triggered by disputes over land seizures and forced demolitions of homes by local governments and developers, arbitrary fees imposed on farmers by local officials, and wage arrears—although a growing number have to do with environmental degradation, corruption, and ethnic conflict.[17]

The ever-escalating number of public protests, large and small, make China's government very nervous . . . and for good reason. In the wake of the Arab Spring and Color Revolutions elsewhere in the world the authorities in China are hypervigilant against uprisings and move quickly to suppress them. Where possible they are broken up peacefully, but sometimes force is used and sometimes lives are lost. The paramilitary People's Armed Police (PAP) are responsible for handling "riots, large-scale violent crimes, and terrorist attacks," and they are backed by local militia, special provincial commando units, military reserves, or (if necessary) People's Liberation Army units.[18] Ministry of Public Security forces number about 25 million nationwide. It is no accident that since 2011 China's internal security budget is actually larger than its military budget! This is all part of what the government refers to as "stability maintenance" (维稳) activities. The new National Security and Counter-Terrorism laws, passed in 2015, signify the government's concern and strengthen its hand in preemption and suppression. This is all part of a much broader crackdown and tightening up of internal security begun in 2009 but significantly strengthened since Xi Jinping came to power in 2012. We will return to this subject in the next chapter, but first let us consider one specific dimension of the problem.

The Volatile Periphery

Among the most acute challenges for the Chinese government to manage over the coming decade are the increasingly unstable border regions of Xinjiang, Tibet, Hong Kong, and Taiwan (Figure 3.4). Xinjiang and Tibet are highly unstable, Hong Kong and Taiwan less so, but all have real potential for major confrontations with Beijing.

The origins of instability have their unique characteristics in each region, but to varying degrees residents in each locale all resent and resist rule by the central government in Beijing. In each case the nub of the problem are the *separate identities* that the residents of these regions possess. These separate identities are of an ethnic and religious nature in Xinjiang and Tibet.[19] In Hong Kong and Taiwan surveys show that there is also an ethnic element, but they have more to do with political identity and suzerainty, owing to the mainland's creeping influence and their histories as autonomous from the regime that rules the mainland.[20] Taiwan polls consistently show that a majority of the island's residents do not consider themselves "Chinese" while recent polls in Hong Kong show that a meager 12.6 percent view themselves as solely "Chinese" (nearly 50 percent see themselves as "Hong Kongers but also Chinese" with 27 percent identifying solely as "Hong Kongers").[21]

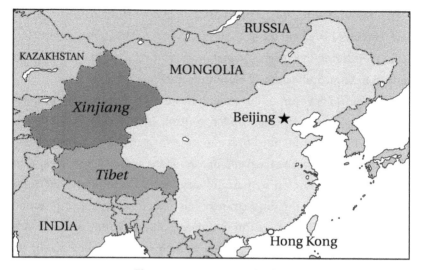

Figure 3.4 Xinjiang and Tibet

In the cases of Xinjiang and Tibet, part of the problem is also caused by the extreme physical repression and persecution Uighurs and Tibetans have experienced at the hands of the security services (beatings, detentions, disappearances, arrests, incarcerations, and demolitions of monasteries and places of worship). In addition to repression, there is also widespread discrimination in employment, religious worship, access to education and legal services, native language teaching, and other ethnic practices denied by the Han Chinese and local government authorities (who are viewed by many as occupiers).

There is a pervasive sense of despair in both Xinjiang and Tibet. In protest, Tibetans have sparked a number of uprisings and have taken to immolating themselves—a total of 147 people from 2009 to mid-2015.[22] In Xinjiang, there have also been numerous uprisings and large-scale loss of life. Major riots erupted in Lhasa in March 2008, Urumqi in July 2009 and May 2014, as well as in Hotan and Kashgar in July 2011. In these cases the protests were ruthlessly suppressed by paramilitary

PAP units, and both cities remain under lockdown and *de facto* martial law. Uighurs have also taken their grievances to the heartland of Han China, engaging in extreme acts of mass terrorism and killing of civilians in Beijing, Shijiazhuang, Kunming, and Guangzhou.

The central government in Beijing has tried various tactics to keep these peripheral territories under control. In Xinjiang and Tibet it has used a combination of economic investment, infrastructure construction, pervasive surveillance by state security agencies, and heavy-handed coercion by paramilitary forces. In the cases of Hong Kong and Taiwan, Beijing's strategy has rested on trying to produce economic dependence on the mainland, plus different political tactics in each place. In Hong Kong, Beijing has worked through its handpicked representatives and the territory's tycoons. This approach has deeply alienated the majority of average Hong Kong citizens. Beijing's alteration of the procedures for electing the Chief Executive in 2017 has also proven deeply divisive, triggering the 2014 "Occupy Central" movement or "umbrella revolution" (Figure 3.5) that lasted for seventy-nine days and brought hundreds of thousands of residents into the streets to protest Beijing's actions.

In the case of Taiwan, Beijing does not have the same political option of working through manipulated elites and officials, given the island's independent and robust democracy. Even the dramatic growth in cross-strait ties and interdependence built in recent years has begun to produce a backlash in Taiwan, with many citizens believing it has produced an undesirable and irreversible dependency on the mainland (exemplified by the "Sunflower Movement" (Figure 3.6) and occupation of the Legislature and Executive Yuan in 2014).

Thus, in both Hong Kong and Taiwan, the evident and secular trend is *away from*—not toward—the mainland and central government. This trend is likely to deepen in future years, with more and more frictions

Figure 3.5 Hong Kong's "Umbrella Revolution"
Source: Flickr.com.

Figure 3.6 Taiwan's Sunflower Movement
Source: Flickr.com.

anticipated in each case. Should the mainland attempt to use force against either territory in an attempt to suppress what it considers "separatist activities," an unpredictable and explosive situation would ensue.

Looking over the horizon into the future, these four territories are likely to become more, and not less, unstable. They will provide an ever-increasing challenge to the central government in Beijing. The situation is already dire. While impossible to measure, my sense is that three of the four (Taiwan being the exception) "live on the brink" of exploding into full-scale civil disobedience and anti-regime activities. Each is a tinderbox waiting to be ignited; indeed, the fuses are already burning. The central government's default response is more and more coercion, in attempts to deter and suppress desires for true autonomy in these "autonomous regions." Nor will attempts to buy passivity through large infrastructure investments work. Instead of the default mode of repression and economic cooptation, if Beijing were wise it would pursue the opposite policies of conciliation, tolerance, and true autonomy. This requires a very different mindset in the Chinese Communist Party than currently exists (see chapter 4).

Civil Society

One of the key social-political issues in China's future will be the evolution of civil society. Civil society is considered to be the totality of civic activities that take place in the community among individual citizens, groups, or organizations *fully autonomous from and not controlled by the state*. In democratic polities civil society is not an issue—it is an intrinsic aspect of how such a society should function. But in authoritarian political systems, like China, it is very much an issue, and a highly political one.

The Chinese government and Communist Party have always had an ambivalent relationship with this domain of social activity since it first began to arise during the 1980s. After the Tiananmen uprising of April–June 1989 and the collapse of East European communism that summer and autumn, CCP leaders were quick to blame these events on a too tolerant attitude toward actors in civil society, notably intellectuals. As the "color revolutions" swept across the post-Soviet space in the mid-1990s, Beijing was quick to blame the West—specifically the United States—for fomenting revolutionary uprisings against sovereign (authoritarian) governments. This led to a decade-long cat-and-mouse game between the Chinese government and various civil-society actors. During this period, the mid-1990s to the mid-2000s, the scope and space for civil society progressively widened. It was not so much that the government encouraged it as various civic actors simply became active in the intermediate space between the individual and the state. To some extent the authorities were tolerant of the growth of civil society, to some extent they tried to control it through cooptation (forming government-organized non-governmental organizations or GONGOs), but to a large extent the rapid enlargement of private civic activities simply outpaced the government's watchful eyes and repressive instruments. As a result, according to Ministry of Civil Affairs statistics, by the end of 2003 there were 1,736 officially centrally registered "social organizations" (社会团体), 142,121 at the local level, and 124,491 "private non-enterprise units."[23] By 2014 the total number continued to mushroom to over 500,000 officially registered with an estimated 1.5 million additional unregistered entities.[24] This included a wide range of advocacy groups—from those promoting HIV/AIDS awareness to entities concerned with migrants' rights, disaster victims, and a wide variety of other worthy causes. Philanthropic charities have begun to germinate even if private giving remains a very underdeveloped concept among China's wealthy classes.

Yet as civil society took root and grew during these years, so too did the party-state's concerns. Beginning around 2009–2010 the central and local governmental authorities began to rein in these proliferating organizations, as part of a broader political tightening and crackdown (see chapter 4). This very much applied to foreign-funded NGOs as well, which had also grown in number and activities. The motivation for the increased concern and control was a growing concern about the potential for a "color" or "jasmine" revolution being triggered by these groups (and their supposed foreign government backers) in China. Some reliable Chinese sources report that Russia's Vladimir Putin was instrumental in getting former President Hu Jintao to crack down on civil society, physically grabbing Hu by the lapel at a Shanghai Cooperation Organization summit and telling him, "If you do not get a grip on these NGOs in China, as we are doing in Russia, you too will have a color revolution!"[25] Hu returned to China and initiated the crackdown, which continues till this day. It has intensified greatly since Xi Jinping came to power in 2012. Between 2012 and 2015 more than 500 activists and dissidents have been arrested and sentenced to prison.[26] Within one fortnight in July 2015 more than 200 "rights lawyers" (attorneys who defend others' rights in the judicial system) were detained as "provocateurs" and "troublemakers."[27] A broad blanket of surveillance has descended over urban China and over cyber China. China's new cyber law is one of four draconian laws passed or in draft form during 2015 (the others being the National Security Law, Counter-Terrorism Law, and Foreign NGO Law) which have given state authorities virtually unlimited legal authority and power to detain, arrest, and imprison citizens who are deemed to be threats to the state. The text of the cyber law makes it unlawful for any "defaming information" to be reposted

500 times or viewed 5,000 times via social media. As a result, large numbers of online writers and bloggers have been detained for "picking quarrels and provoking trouble" online. The National Security Law gives the internal security and judicial organs broad authority to control and repress a wide range of domestic actors.[28] The NGO Law will make it next to impossible for foreign NGOs to operate in China, and even makes difficult normal academic exchanges and activities involving foreign universities. The Counter-Terrorism Law, among other things, gives legal authority to the government to intrude on the private lives and communications of all 1.39 billion citizens. Taken together, these new laws take to a new level the legal scope of state control and repression in China.

The struggle between the party-state and society over civil society (and the public sphere more broadly) is only going to grow more contentious over time, and will become one of the key pressure points on Party rule over the next decade. The party-state is currently trying to put the proverbial genie back in the bottle, but this retrograde effort reveals a number of problems. First, civil society may already be too widely developed to be controlled. It is like the game of "Whack-a-Mole": whenever one is hit, others pop up. Second, information technologies—particularly social media—are probably too widely used to be effectively controlled. Third, the attempts to control and thwart these interactions and to prosecute innocent citizens only further alienate society from the state. It is ultimately a losing battle for the party-state, and only reveals its profound *insecurity* in the face of normal social activities.

The battleground over the next decade will be in the cities, in cyberspace, in intellectual publications, and in university classrooms—and the Party is fighting a losing war. The only alternative, as described in the next chapter at greater length, is for the Party to return to its more open, tolerant, and liberal policies of the 1998–2008 period. If it does so, civil society will flourish. No doubt this would increase criticisms of the Party and government, but a *secure* ruling Party elite could take a more expansive and positive-sum approach by listening to—rather than repressing—such criticisms. It might even serve to strengthen Party rule. But, at present and given what we know of the mindset of Xi Jinping and current Party leaders, there is zero interest in returning to this more tolerant and liberal path. As a result, we can expect tensions within and over civil society to steadily grow more and more strained . . . until there is a breaking point.

Urbanization

Another significant future challenge for China is increasing urbanization (城镇化), which is a very high priority of the government and particularly of Premier Li Keqiang during his tenure in office (which ends in 2022). In March 2014 Li unveiled the "National New-Type Urbanization Plan," the nation's first-ever official urbanization blueprint.[29] Probably no government in history has devised such a comprehensive orchestrated urbanization scheme on such a grand scale—involving issues of land and buildings, public and private transportation, communications, public services, finances, ecology, food, labor, governance, and other facets of urban planning.[30] China spends up to $400 billion a year on buildings, putting up 28 billion square feet of new residential property annually. It is forecast to account for 40 percent of global construction in the next ten years.[31] The government's goal is to have 60 percent of the population living in urban areas by 2020—requiring the relocation of 260 million rural inhabitants, creating 110 million new jobs, permanently absorbing 150 million migrants already living in metropolitan areas and providing them with legitimate rights for dwelling, education, healthcare, and other basic social services. By 2030 over 1 billion Chinese—70 percent of the nation's population—will be living in cities, if all goes according to plan. This is an ambitious and enormous undertaking that no government or society has ever attempted. If successful, it will contribute positively to two key elements of the new macro-economic growth model by creating a new pool of labor for the services sector and stimulating consumer spending.

China's urbanization has been a steady process since the reform era began in 1978 (Figure 3.7). At that time only 18 percent (172 million people) lived in urban areas—today slightly more than half of the national population (54 percent or 731 million) are categorized as urban. This steady increase was the result of three processes: rural-to-urban migration; massive building of new urban infrastructure; and rezoning (physically expanding the boundaries) of cities.

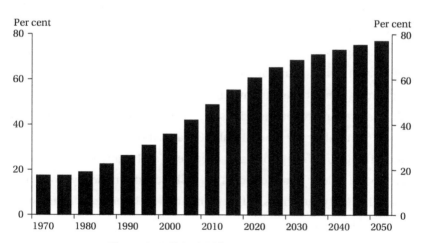

Figure 3.7 China's Urbanization Growth
Source: Australian Treasury Department.

The three main drivers of urbanization in the future, according to Premier Li Keqiang, will be to give urban residency (*hukou*) to 100 million migrants who currently live in cities (an amnesty, in effect); rebuilding dilapidated parts of existing urban areas, where an additional 100 million currently live; and urbanizing an additional 100 million in the central and western regions of the country.[32] This "300 million initiative" will account for the additional 16 percent due to become urban dwellers between now and 2030.

The sheer magnitude of China's cities is hard to grasp. Today there are five cities with a population over 10 million; fourteen cities over 5 million; and 41 cities of 2 million or more.[33] By 2025, McKinsey & Company estimates, 46 of the world's 200 largest cities will be in China.[34] There are plans to turn the greater Pearl River Delta—including Guangzhou, Shenzhen, and Zhuhai—into one enormous megacity (都市花) of 42 million people,[35] and the Beijing-Tianjin-Hebei triangle (known as Jing-Jin-Ji) into an even larger one covering 82,000 square miles and a total population of 130 million people.[36] The new strategy to create megalopolises is a shift from just a few years ago when the government's priority was to develop small and medium-sized cities.[37]

Creating "ecocities" and "green urbanization" are another part of the government's plan—an appropriate goal given the environmental catastrophe that besets many Chinese cities. Less than 1 percent of China's five hundred largest cities meet the PM2.5 air quality standards recommended by the World Health Organization.[38] This is not the first time that China has prioritized ecocities—ambitious plans in 2008–2009 were quietly abandoned as air pollution dramatically worsened in Beijing and other cities. While plans are well-intended, one must be skeptical in this realm.

Urbanization is not only utilitarian. It also involves architectural aesthetics. As architectural scholar Li Shiqiao discusses in his book

Understanding the Chinese City, Chinese urban planning involves distinctive approaches.[39] Land usage for public space, the use of building materials, design shapes (preference for rectangles), and *fengshui* (the practice of geomancy) all distinguish Chinese cities. While much urban construction in China lacks architectural imagination, continuing the unimaginative East German apartment block tradition or the "fortress" design so prevalent in Chinese government buildings, some major eastern cities boast bold designs, such as the National Center for Performing Arts, Shanghai Opera House, "Bird's Nest" Olympic stadium, the CCTV tower in Beijing, Suzhou Art Museum, Guangzhou's Circle Building (the "Copper Coin"), or a variety of futuristic glass buildings that dot the urban landscape. Many of these were designed by foreign architects. Apparently not everyone in China appreciates these contemporary designs, though. None other than paramount leader Xi Jinping sharply criticized *avant garde* buildings as "weird architecture" (奇怪建筑), and he called for a halt to it in a speech on October 15, 2014. In Xi's view, architecture should "be like sunshine from the blue sky and the breeze in spring that will inspire minds, warm hearts, cultivate taste, and clean up undesirable workstyles."[40]

Urbanization also has a political dimension. As the China scholar Jeremy Wallace argues, the generally planned—not ad hoc—urban development of China's largest cities has won the regime a large degree of support from urban dwellers, particularly the middle class.[41] The relative lack of urban slums, beggars, and crime sets Chinese cities apart from most other developing countries. Still, chronic problems such as traffic gridlock and air pollution drive citizens to demand improvement. Wallace also notes that, ironically, cities become magnets for protest and remonstration against the state.

In sum, China's plans for urban development are some of the most intriguing and potentially profound for the country's future. For a people who have been tied to agricultural land and farming for centuries, urbanization represents not only a huge physical shift but also a psychological change. Clans who have lived next to each other for eternity are being dispersed to new locales with new neighbors. The sheer size and number of China's cities ensures perpetual stresses on insufficient public services, while the hard infrastructure inevitably degrades over time. On the positive side, urbanization will transform the labor market (especially in services), unlock new waves of consumer spending, and provide improved daily life for over 1 billion people.

Migration and the Labor Market

China's urbanization is intricately tied to the issue of rural-urban migration and the *hukou* (户口) problem. There are an estimated 200 million migrants currently living in cities and, according to the Development Research Center of the State Council, in-migration has accounted for 56.1 percent of urban population growth between 2001 and 2012.[42] This large influx of rural migrants has really strained municipal governments to provide housing and basic social services for the migrants. Of course, technically, these people are not entitled to local services if they do not possess a *hukou* (registration) there. This includes, in theory at least, attending local schools or universities.

The *hukou* system is a leftover from the Maoist era, when the communist government sought to control the movement of all citizens.[43] It was a key instrument in the totalitarian toolbox. During the reform era the system progressively broke down and caused a massive problem of a "floating population" (流动人口) of 200+ million people. China's National Bureau of Statistics estimated that, in 2015, 278 million people resided somewhere else than their official *hukou*.[44] As a result there have been never-ending debates about how to reform the *hukou* system, dismantle it in part, or whether to abolish it altogether. Keeping it in place certainly constrains the development of a real national labor market. While it would be most rational to abolish it, the government has resisted this path so far and instead tinkers with various experiments and alternative plans for reform of the system. To this end, on July 30, 2014, the CCP Politburo approved the new *Guidelines to Step-up Reform of the Household Registration System*. The new guidelines unified the national registration system, doing away with the two-tier urban and rural system that created, in effect, apartheid. The new system still stops short of giving amnesty to those migrants already residing illegally in cities, although the new guidelines stipulated that restrictions on access to public services should be relaxed.[45] While a step in the right direction, it remains to be seen if the new system will work or, more important, how urban governments will pay for the increased demand on public services.

Another dimension is that China's surplus rural labor, which has been an engine to national economic growth, has now peaked—passing what is known as the Lewis Turning Point (when wages are no longer suppressed due to the excess pool of rural labor that flows out of farming and into the industrial sector). As a result, wages are steadily rising in both rural and urban areas. This is affecting a core element of China's post-1978 growth model: low-end manufacturing based on low wages for migrant labor. The aging of the population is also contributing to the gradual shrinking of the labor force as the "baby boomers" born in the 1960s–1970s, who powered the post-reform boom, age. Let us look at this more closely.

Demographic Transition

Of all the multiple social challenges we catalogue in this chapter, perhaps the most profound—yet quietest—factor shaping China's future is its demographic transition from a young to an aging society (Figure 3.8). The size of the country's population aged 60 and above will increase dramatically, growing by 100 million in just fifteen years—from 200 million in 2015 to over 300 million by 2030—and a projected 450 million by 2050. The number of families with only one child, the vast majority of the population, only underscores the challenge of supporting the growing numbers of elderly Chinese. Indeed, increased spending obligations created by the aging of the population will not only shift resources away from investment and production; they will also test the government's ability to meet rising demands for benefits and services. In combination, the declining labor supply and increased public and private spending obligations will result in a society that has not been seen in China before.

Japan's economic stagnation, closely related to the aging of its population, serves as a ready reference. China's low fertility rate (1.7) is now below the replacement level and assures continually declining numbers of new entrants into the labor force, despite the loosening of the one-child policy restrictions in 2013 and its abolition in 2015.

The situation is stark and the implications serious for China. The "demographic dividend" is over. As demographer Wang Feng of the University of California–Irvine aptly describes the situation, "The aging of China's population represents a *crisis* (emphasis added) because its arrival is imminent and inevitable, because its ramifications are huge and long-lasting, and because its effects will be hard to reverse. Political legitimacy in China over the past three decades has been built around fast economic growth, which in turn has relied on a cheap and

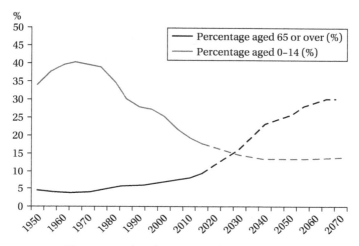

Figure 3.8 China's Demographic Projections
Source: United Nations World Population Prospects (2015).

willing young labor force. An aging labor force will compel changes in this economic model and may make political rule more difficult."[46] Wang Feng further argues, "As the population ages, the momentum of negative growth will eventually predominate."[47]

This is not only a future problem; it has arrived. According to China's National Bureau of Statistics, the working-age population has already begun to shrink—from 941 million in 2011 to 916 million in 2014.[48] Between 2016 and 2026 the number of workers aged twenty to twenty-nine will fall by nearly 25 percent from 200 million to 150 million; the drop will be even sharper for those aged twenty to twenty-four.[49] By 2050 the labor force is estimated by McKinsey & Company to contract by 11 percent.[50] These trends are going to have profound implications for China's economy.

Thus, of all the various factors affecting China's future and particularly the country's economic growth prospects, China's demographic transition is perhaps the most fundamental and structural. Even if

China were to hypothetically have another baby boom over the next ten or twenty years (highly doubtful also because of the severe male-female sex ratio imbalance), it would be thirty to forty years before it would affect the economy. By then China's economy will be far less dependent on labor than it is now. In addition to squeezing the economy, China's aging society is going to place enormous strains on the "public goods" provided by the state and non-state actors.

Provision of Public Goods

Another huge future challenge for China and the government at all levels will be the provision of so-called public goods (public services) to the population. This is a challenge not only because of the size of the population and its aging demographic profile but also because the widespread experience of other countries has been that as they grow in prosperity citizens begin to care more about (and expect) qualitative improvements in their lives, not only material creature comforts. This is the case in China too, as many public opinion polls indicate.

Public goods include a very wide range of services provided to societies (normally by governments but also by private sector actors). These include things as diverse as national defense and security, police and crime prevention, traffic lights, public transportation, food safety standards, building codes, and so on. While China has made much progress in recent years in improving its provision of public goods (notably healthcare), it still lags considerably behind Organization for Economic Cooperation and Development (OECD) countries. For example, in 2011 OECD countries spent an average of 7.7 percent of their GDP on healthcare, while China spent only 2.9 percent; OECD spending on education was 5.7 percent of GDP while China's was just

3.6 percent in 2010.[51] In China's case, I am going to briefly discuss several areas that will be particularly salient over the next decade: healthcare, pensions, education, the environment, and energy usage.

Healthcare

Healthcare provision has been a success story over the past few years. After a three-decade progressive decline during the reform era, when the state-supported system steadily atrophied, the Hu Jintao–Wen Jiabao government undertook a major initiative in 2009 to rebuild the system and provide universal and comprehensive healthcare to the whole population by 2020.[52] The effort has been a stunning success, as just five years later 95 percent of the population enjoyed some health insurance coverage. This is a dramatic reversal in an extremely short period, as 80 percent of households paid entirely out of their own pockets as recently as 2007.[53] This stunning turnaround was the result of significant injections of central government subsidies. Between 2009 and 2011 the government pumped 1.24 trillion RMB into the healthcare system.[54] Total healthcare spending is estimated to rise from $357 billion in 2011 to $1 trillion in 2020, according to the international consulting firm McKinsey & Company.[55]

The new healthcare initiative is part of the government's "five guarantees" to its citizens: food, clothing, medical care, housing, and burial expenses. The healthcare system overhaul also includes the construction of many new local hospitals and neighborhood clinics, training mobile medical workers to roam the countryside, infectious disease prevention and personal hygiene education programs, improved neonatal care, extended care for migrants, and stricter regulation of pharmaceutical manufacturing and sale.

So the provision of healthcare—accessibility and affordability—has gone from a bad-news to a good-news story over the past few years. If sustainable, it will have a significant positive impact on care for the elderly and provision of services for China's growing urban population. This said, health insurance provided has been partial coverage (not 100 percent) and most citizens continue to face significant out-of-pocket expenses and limits on the quality of care they can receive.

Overhauling the healthcare system is also intended to pay macroeconomic dividends. One reason for the excessively high savings rate in China has been the citizenry's financial fears about their health and how to support themselves in retirement. Prior to the post-2009 reforms, as noted above, 80 percent of the population reportedly had no health insurance whatsoever. Personal savings were the only way to pay for regular, emergency, or catastrophic healthcare. Now, with that funded by the state, these savings are freed up (in theory) to be pumped into the economy for other consumption purposes—thus contributing to one main pillar of the Third Plenum economic reform plan.

Pensions

Similarly, the government should also be credited with simultaneously overhauling and funding China's badly broken retirement pension system. This too was a chronic crisis looming on the horizon as the massive retirement threshold neared in 2014–2015. Personal savings were being hoarded for the proverbial "rainy day" as nearly 80 percent of the population also had no form of funding for their retirements other than savings. Thus, beginning around 2008, the government began its overhaul program, established a national pension administration, and injected greater funds into the system. The World Bank helped design the program.[56] By 2011 pension expenditures had risen to 1.28 trillion RMB, almost three times more than 2006.[57] As a result, Chinese over the age of sixty enrolled in the pension plan doubled from 30 percent in 2009 to 60 percent in 2012.[58] This included 290 million urban workers. In 2014 the State Council further revised the pension system, establishing, for the first time, a unified nationwide system that would cover all "non-working urban and rural residents" (including migrants). By the end of the year, the total of urban residents covered under the new pension insurance scheme totaled 501.07 million nationwide, according to official statistics.[59]

Nonetheless, as in the American Social Security system, projections are that there will not be enough public money to fund the system as the tsunami of baby boomers retire *en masse*. A Bank of China/ Deutsche Bank study estimates that the shortfall will be $10.9 trillion by 2033 (38.7 percent of GDP), while the Chinese Academy of Social Sciences estimates that by 2050 there will be a $128 trillion gap.[60] Thus, while the pension problem seems to have been ameliorated in the short term, it remains a long-term financial problem that haunts China's future.

Higher Education

Another key public good for China's future is higher education. Recall from chapter 2 that innovation is *the key* to China's future, and one of the two central elements of the government's macroeconomic development strategy—as such, higher education is the key incubator of creativity and new inventions (private corporate R&D plays a secondary role). Yet education is, and will likely remain, one of the main bottlenecks holding back China's future development. There are a number of dimensions to the existing problems afflicting China's higher education system: over-bureaucratization and a too-close relationship between the party-state and universities; the politicization of subject content taught; curriculum and pedagogical impediments; the research culture; faculty training and recruitment; and the returnee problem.

It is no secret that China's universities are far from being world class (only three mainland universities—Peking, Tsinghua, and Fudan—rank in the top 100 on the *Times Higher Education* global rankings). Nor is it a secret that China's leaders aspire to having a world-class system. Various reforms have been under way since the mid-1990s and enormous amounts of funding have flowed into the university sector, but with minimal qualitative progress to date. The system has been structurally reorganized several times on the premise of concentrating resources in a select number of universities in order to produce synergies of faculty expertise that, in theory, would be innovative. This is like applying an industrial policy approach to education.

The first wave of reforms was the so-called "Project 211," which aimed at building one hundred "key point" universities (重点大学) by the turn of the twenty-first century (hence the 211 designator). If the first phase was aimed at breadth, the second phase concentrated on depth. The second wave was triggered by former president Jiang Zemin's speech on the hundredth anniversary of Peking University on May 4, 1998, when Jiang proclaimed "China must have a number of world-class universities." Dubbed the "985 Project" (for 1998, May), the plan identified nine "core universities" (the C-9) plus thirty other priority institutions that were to be favored with funding and faculty. A key element of this plan was to create a range of incentivized programs to attract Chinese who graduated with advanced degrees abroad to return to China and teach in C-9 institutions. While the foreign returnee rate has improved in recent years, it still remains very low. Chinese Ministry of Education statistics show that after reaching an all-time low of 24.3 percent students returning after graduation in

2004, the figure has gradually grown to 36.5 percent in 2011 (the most recent available figures).[61] But this means that 63.5 percent of Chinese students who go abroad do not return! By the 2013–2014 academic year a total of 459,800 Chinese students were studying abroad, according to the Ministry of Education.[62] Think about these figures for a moment: more than 2 million of China's best and brightest go abroad for study and only a little more than *one-third* return home! This is a damning indictment of China's higher education system in two ways—the total number of those who go abroad and the dismal number of those who return. But it speaks to more than just China's educational system, as it is an indicator of broader dissatisfaction with the restrictions that result from the political system in China, as well as very personal issues such as salary levels, affordability of housing, the environment, and perhaps above all the desire to raise children in the West. We will return to this theme in the next chapter when we consider the weaknesses in China's political system, but note here this conundrum: How is China to become an innovative society if the best and brightest remain overseas?

At any rate, Project 211 never really took off as envisioned because it was largely dependent on local governments funding it, and local governments were cash-strapped and had other priorities. The 985 Project did produce better dividends, as several of the Core-9 have emerged as national leaders, with three on the global top 100 list.[63] What these reforms have done, however, is to create a multi-tiered system with thirty-nine institutions under Project 985, dozens of Project 211 institutions, and the remaining 2000+ institutions being run by local governments or private (民办) entities.[64] Through this expanded system, higher education has become much more available to millions who could never dream of a college education before. Over the past two decades enrollments have steadily expanded—in 2013 Chinese institutions of higher education had a total enrollment of 34.6 million![65] This is a significant accomplishment that no other developing country has been able to come close to achieving. But the challenge for China going forward is not the quantity of students in the higher educational system, but the quality of the instruction.

The main problems here are curriculum and pedagogy. The curriculum in Chinese universities includes too many required political courses on Marxism, history of China's Communist Party, and so on, but it is also skewed toward courses in applied rather than basic research and methodologies. Chinese students are taught what to think and how to think. The former is bad enough, but the latter is the real problem. There are several interrelated facets here. First, after several thousand years of tradition, Chinese pedagogy still emphasizes rote memorization of required knowledge and "correct thought." This information is learned by students in the classroom and through textbooks that provide all the questions and all the correct answers (in multiple choice format). Doing well on examinations is therefore a pure process of memorization. This includes verbatim memorization of key Communist Party canons. There is little emphasis in Chinese higher education on critical thinking or independent judgment, or the possibility that there may be multiple plausible explanations for a phenomenon. There is only one "correct" answer and deviation from it is penalized. There is no instruction in hypothesis formulation and testing, or the logic that underlies it. There are no essay questions on exams where students are evaluated on their reasoning and independent judgments. There is precious little opportunity for students to speak in class, to question their teachers, to make presentations or work in groups and solve problems jointly. There are no individualized tutorials in which students enter into intellectual dialogue with their professors. And so on.

It is thus no wonder that Chinese institutions of higher education are not incubators of innovation and invention. It is no wonder that so many Chinese parents—including the nation's top leaders—seek to send their single child abroad for college. It is no wonder that such a small percentage return. Until the pedagogy of Chinese educational institutions is completely overhauled and replaced with the Western-style emphasis on individualized learning, independent and critical thinking, basic instead of applied research, and hypothesis-based analysis, China's universities will continue to be mediocre at best.

There is also the related and widespread problem of academic corruption. This is mainly manifest among faculty with respect to promotion criteria—which are not rigorous, and not sufficiently based on publications, peer review, or originality. Professors are too often promoted because of the time they have been on staff, for some paltry publications published in Chinese journals rather than international peer-reviewed ones, because of favoritism, or because they bribe those in positions to promote them. It is a very corrupt system, which one education expert appropriately describes as a "toxic academic culture."[66]

The problem also affects the falsification of dissertations and degrees. As technocracy has taken hold in the political system, many officials nowadays seek a PhD on their resume and somehow manage to produce dissertations at one of China's 2,800 Party schools or regular universities. This includes paramount leader Xi Jinping himself, who was awarded a PhD in Law (LLD) from prestigious Tsinghua University in 2002 for a dissertation entitled "A Tentative Study of China's Rural Marketization." However, analyses of Xi's thesis apparently revealed multiple instances of plagiarism.[67] Dissertations in China are frequently ghostwritten. The plagiarism problem travels when Chinese students go abroad for study (to be fair, students from other nations are also prone to this). Falsification of credentials and ghost-taking foreign university entrance exams such as TOEFEL, ACT, SAT, GRE, GMAT, and LSAT is increasingly commonplace. Some Chinese students who supposedly score high are then admitted— only to arrive in the United States unable to speak or write English or without the essential academic skills to survive. The U.S.-based education consulting firm WholeRen Education found that 8,000 Chinese students had been dismissed from American high schools and universities during 2013–2015. Of these, 23 percent were expelled for plagiarism and cheating while 57 percent were terminated from their programs for poor academic performance.[68]

All of these problems will continue to impact China's higher educational system well into the future. The difficulties are deep, structural, bureaucratic, cultural, and political. Throwing money at the university system in an attempt to buy innovation, like building infrastructure, will only produce very marginal returns for R&D (mainly in the sciences and engineering).

While Chinese cultural biases against individualism and in favor of rote learning are traditional, and predate communist rule, the core problem with Chinese education is the CCP-led political system and the extreme degree to which it stifles the entire intellectual sphere in China. Until the controls are substantially loosened, or the political system is changed entirely, Chinese universities and intellectuals will never be able to realize their great potential and become world class. Therefore, this will be a major impediment to China's economic development, insofar as creativity and innovation are critical to propelling China forward into the future.

Environment and Energy

China's environment is another key factor impinging on its future.[69] Quite simply, China's environment is the world's worst. This includes diminishing (and polluted) water resources, life-threatening and cancer-causing air pollution, desertification, deforestation, climate change, inefficient energy usage, and so on. It directly and negatively affects human health, economic growth, and the planet's global warming. It is also potentially a volatile political issue.

The country now has a number of dubious environmental distinctions.[70] In 2007 China surpassed the United States as the world's largest emitter of carbon dioxide (CO_2). In 2009 China's share of global CO_2 emissions measured 6,319 million tons, 21.4 percent of the world's total.[71] At that rate by 2020 China will be spewing 14.2 billion tons of greenhouse gasses into the atmosphere. China's sulphur dioxide emissions are also the highest in the world. As a result, China chokes on air pollution—accounting for sixteen of the world's twenty most polluted cities and twenty of the world's thirty worst cases.[72] Air pollution and acid rain (a combination of sulphur dioxide and nitrogen oxide) from China are also serious problems affecting the Korean peninsula and Japan to the east and Hong Kong to the south. Polluted rivers in southern China that flow into the Mekong River similarly affect downstream Laos and Vietnam. Pollution is also a significant constraint on economic growth. The World Bank estimates it costs about $100 billion per year or 5.8 percent of GDP.

Water contamination is also pervasive—an estimated 70 percent of Chinese rivers and lakes are contaminated. According to China's Ministry of Environmental Protection, 43.2 percent of state-monitored rivers were classified as Grade 4 or worse in 2010, meaning their water was unsuitable for human contact, while 75 percent of China's lakes were categorized Grade 5 (highly polluted).[73] According to the World Bank, an estimated 300 million rural residents are exposed to nonpotable water,[74] while another study estimated that 90 percent of urban ground water is contaminated.[75] China's own Geological Survey estimates that half of the country's ground water is contaminated.[76] Many rivers and arteries have experienced serious lead, mercury, and other chemical spills. The extensive use of chemical fertilizers and pesticides in agriculture, combined with industrial waste and raw sewage, account for the main sources of river and lake contamination. In 2005, the Songhua River, which flows through northeastern Heilongjiang Province, registered benzene levels 108 times higher than national standards as a result of an upstream chemical plant explosion—resulting in an eighty-kilometer-long downriver toxic slick of an estimated 100 tons of benzene. Chemicals not only leak into the groundwater table and rivers, they also explode on land. A massive chemical explosion in the Binhai Industrial Zone of Tianjin on August 17, 2015, that killed 150 people and injured 700 while torching a several-mile circumference, was catalyzed by 3,000 tons of stored hazardous chemicals, including 700 tons of deadly sodium cyanide. While the scale of the catastrophe in Tianjin was unprecedented, environmental accidents are far from unusual. According to Chinese official statistics, more than 68,000 were killed in such accidents in 2014—an average of almost 200 per day![77]

An even greater threat is water scarcity in much of China. Two-thirds of China's 660 largest cities are reported to be water-stressed, where most of the water supply depends on ground water pumped from aquifers—which are drying up and being depleted due to rapid salinization of soil (the situation is particularly acute on the North China Plain, where eleven provinces face a severe water crisis).[78] The water table is falling by 1.5 percent per year. The World Bank reports that average annual water availability in China is only 1,850 cubic meters per person—less than one-quarter of the world average.[79]

The land is also degrading. Up to 90 percent of China's grasslands are eroding, with desertification now afflicting one-third of China's land mass, forest resources are being depleted (also contributing to ozone depletion), while China's wetlands have reportedly been reduced by 60 percent.[80]

Glacial melt on the Qinghai-Tibetan Plateau is another serious problem. Himalayan glaciers are melting at a rapid rate, having already shrunk by 21 percent. This prospect has profound and dangerous implications, as the Hindu Kush glaciers feed all seven of Asia's great rivers—the Yellow, Yangzi, Mekong, Salween, Indus, Ganges, and Brahmaputra—affecting the Indian subcontinent, Myanmar and Indochina, and eastern China. If there was one transnational environmental issue in Asia calling out for multinational collaboration, it is this one.[81]

To deal with its pervasive environmental degradation China has taken a number of proactive regulatory steps. Since the passage of the first Environmental Protection Law in 1979, China has passed more than 40 environmental protection laws and a large number of state regulations.[82] Since the Third Plenum of 2013 the Premier, Li Keqiang, has declared "war on pollution" and the government has released a series of new anti-pollution measures. The Environmental Protection Law has been thoroughly revised. In May 2014 the State Council issued the "Notice on Assessment Performance Related to Air Pollution Targets"—a series of regulations that ties cadre performance assessments to meeting air pollution reduction targets. Similarly, in April 2014, the National People's Congress Standing Committee approved an amendment to the Environmental Protection Law that ensures (in theory) that local government officials be held accountable should "serious environmental events" occur in their jurisdiction or if they are found to be intentionally hiding or covering up any relevant information concerning such environmental events. Several provinces (led by Shandong) have adopted the PM2.5 air pollution monitoring mechanism and several municipalities (led by Tianjin) have dramatically raised "pollutant discharge fees" for firms that exceed regulated levels. Hebei province has also closed and moved a number of outdated steel, cement, and coal-burning factories. And the Ministry of the Environment has issued new emissions standards for tin, antimony, mercury, and other chemicals discharged into the ground or water systems. These are all encouraging and important new initiatives—but, like all past environmental measures (of which China has no shortage), the key will lie in implementation and enforcement.

The government and private industry have taken a broad range of initiatives to cut emissions and transition the economy increasingly to alternative renewable sources.[83] At the United Nations Summit on Climate Change in September 2009, former President Hu Jintao announced a series of initiatives that included reduction of CO_2 to 1.5 billion tons by 2020 (a 17 percent reduction in carbon intensity over 2005 levels), expanding forests to cover 40 million hectares, and increasing the share of nonfossil fuels in primary energy consumption to around 15 percent by 2020.[84] At his summit meeting with U.S. President Obama in November 2014, Xi Jinping advanced China's previous commitments to cut CO_2 emissions by agreeing that China's would "peak around 2030" (note: American emissions peaked in 2007).

In trying to meet its energy demand, China is building twenty-seven new nuclear power plants (with thirteen already in operation). This will go a long way toward meeting the 85 percent increase in projected electricity demand by 2020. New building construction is similarly supposed to meet higher energy efficiency standards. The government has also set higher efficiency standards for coal plants, shutting down many older plants and mines producing less than 30,000 tons per year, while also trying to eliminate the personal burning of bituminous "soft" coal during winter. Bio fuels are also being promoted (China is now the world's third largest ethanol producer). China's solar energy industry is booming; in 2007 it became the world's largest producer of photovoltaic cells. In 2009 China became the world's top wind turbine producer, and is now the world's fifth largest consumer of wind power.[85] Altogether, for 2015–2030, China has pledged to invest $6.4 trillion (40 trillion RMB) into improved energy efficiency, nonfossil fuels, and low carbon technologies.[86]

Despite these impressive, indeed unprecedented, green commitments to become more energy efficient and environmentally safe, China's energy usage does not portend well for the future. China has an insatiable appetite for energy, which is growing by the year and decade. In 2010 China became the world's largest total energy consumer, accounting for nearly half of the world's energy consumption growth over the previous decade. Driving China's energy demand has been heavy industry and the needed inputs—particularly steel, cement, and aluminum—which account for more than two-thirds of total energy demand (China is the world's leading producer in these sectors). However, this import demand for natural resources will certainly slow (and already is slowing) as the economy contracts. China's imports of iron ore and other commodities fell off considerably as its industrial economy contracted during 2015.[87]

While China is doing its best to tap domestic reserves, it is increasingly dependent on overseas sources of supply. In 1993 China crossed the threshold to being a net importer of oil, and it is now the world's largest. China's oil consumption has been growing about 8 percent per year since 2002.[88] The International Energy Agency projects that by 2030 China's oil demand will rise to 16.6 million barrels per day and its imports will reach 12.5 million bb/d.[89] At this rate of continued growth in demand for fossil fuels, China's energy usage will continue to be a major strain on the environment, domestically and internationally.

Pathways to China's Social Future

All of these public goods—healthcare, pensions, education, environment, and energy—are going to be increasingly important to China's future over the next ten to twenty years and beyond. Recent reforms in healthcare and pensions portend well for the future, but higher education, energy, and the environment are all major trouble spots on the horizon.

The possible pathways to the future are as complex as Chinese society itself. Generally speaking, I see political variables as determining effective management of the social variables—which, in turn, will determine economic development. *None* of the social and economic challenges we have identified and discussed in the previous two chapters can be effectively addressed or resolved without a significant political loosening and liberalization.

The Limits of Hard Authoritarianism and Neo-Totalitarianism

As was the case concerning the economic challenges, a continuation of current government and Party policies (Hard Authoritarianism) is a recipe for further *social volatility*. As is the case with the economy, the lack of liberalization and political loosening will only exacerbate the multiple existing social problems discussed in this chapter.

Chinese society will become *more*—not less—unstable with the stubborn continuation of repressive policies. An attempted return to Neo-Totalitarian policies would only add greater stresses to society and in state-society relations.

This is certainly the case with what I describe as the "volatile periphery." Absent a 180-degree change in policy by Beijing, one of these days Tibet and/or Xinjiang will explode in widespread upheaval against the Hans and Chinese Communist Party rule. It may already be too late for change, the scars are too deep. Tibet and Xinjiang seethe with hostility and frustration. Hong Kong is not far behind, although the problems are different and not quite as acute. Taiwan is also rebelling against its growing relationship with—and dependence on—the mainland. If Beijing thinks it will break the will of the citizens of all four localities through sheer coercion and obstinacy of policy, it is sorely mistaken. Cracking down is not the way to win over these peoples on the periphery.

I see a similar situation with respect to civil society, with the regime turning toward harsh repressive tactics since 2009. In this instance, though, the situation is much more difficult for the security services and party-state to contain. The sheer spread of social media is ultimately beyond the government's control. The internet, while under government control, may eventually overwhelm the ability to block it—or new ways will be devised to get around the Great Firewall. But more important than these tactical factors is the reality that the citizenry of China have grown accustomed to their newfound (relative) freedoms, and will likely resist a return to China's totalitarian past. In my opinion, the regime is playing with fire here—by cracking down, especially on the middle class, it is sowing the seeds of greater resentment and thus bringing the entire political system to an even more brittle (and possibly breaking) point.

The Need for Soft Authoritarianism or Semi-Democracy

Only a return to more open and tolerant Soft Authoritarianism or a bold transition to a Semi-Democratic political system will effectively address China's multiple social problems.

When it comes to public goods, a continuation of the status quo and current policies with respect to education and the environment is constrained by political factors. Higher education needs a near-complete overhaul based on a liberal model of education—but this, in turn, requires a significant liberalization of the political system. Even the political liberalization pursued from 1998 to 2008 (see chapter 4) is insufficient to bring about the needed changes to curriculum and pedagogy in the classroom. Similarly, the environmental disaster that is China today is directly attributable to the economic model the government has fostered—which is directly attributable to the intrinsic need to constantly grow the economy at the maximum level possible in order to win the political support of the population (as the party-state only has one other significant source of support: nationalism). So, I see these two social problems—higher education and environment—as also directly linked to politics. When it comes to the other two public goods discussed—healthcare and pensions—we saw that they too were time bombs waiting to explode—until the government (to its credit) proactively launched major new reform initiatives costing trillions to revamp and subsidize each sector. If this cannot be sustained, the time bombs will begin ticking again.

When it comes to the other major social problems discussed in this chapter, social stratification and urbanization, these are also essentially questions of political economy. The former is a consequence of past government policies while the latter is an ongoing policy of unprecedented dimensions. We identified the steps that the government is taking to alleviate the pressures in both domains—primarily reform of the *hukou* system and providing adequate housing and healthcare in China's cities, as well as transfer payments to try and narrow (or stabilize) income gaps. These are positive steps. But time will tell if they are enough to cope with the totality of the problem.

We also identified some social variables that are out of the control of the party-state, particularly the aging of society and the massive wave of retirements already under way. The government cannot do anything about this as it is a natural and long-term trend—but the authorities at all levels are already feeling the consequences of it. The initiatives to fund and reconstruct the healthcare and pension systems are a direct consequence of the demographic transition under way. Here, for once, the government anticipated the problem and did something about it before it was too late.

Thus, on balance, without political liberalization (Soft Authoritarianism or Semi-Democracy) Chinese society is only going to become more and more unstable and unpredictable. At some point, some—or several—of the elements we have identified will "snap." And when that happens, given the deep-seated frustrations existing across society, it will likely trigger horizontal ripple effects across the country. So far the authorities have been able to control, co-opt, and contain the "nodes" of protests when they break out—but this cannot be assured in the future. And let us remember that Chinese society has a historical propensity to erupt in large-scale social upheaval every twenty-five to thirty years or so. It is overdue.

On the other hand, if political reforms are introduced it could well alleviate many of the social stresses, stabilize the country, and buy the regime more time in power. Let us now turn to assessing the future of China's polity.

4

China's Polity

The effectiveness of how well China's party-state addresses the broad range of economic and social challenges outlined in the two previous chapters will depend in large part on the nature of China's political system. China's future will be largely determined by whether China's ruling Communist Party loosens, tightens, or maintains its current controls over various elements in the polity, economy, and society. In order to understand these possible alternatives for the future (which are considered at the end of this chapter) it is important to understand the political situation today and how it has evolved to this point. China's current political state of Hard Authoritarianism has existed since 2009. It was different before that time, and to anticipate future possibilities it is thus important to understand this background and evolution.

China's Recent Political Evolution

China's political orientation has passed, in my view, through five broad phases over the past thirty years. These are captured in Figure 4.1.

Throughout these three decades there is an apparent oscillating pattern of political opening and tightening—what is known among scholars of Chinese politics as the *fang-shou cycle* (放收周期). This schizophrenic pattern reveals that there have long been two contending

Period	Political Orientation
1985–1989	Liberal Neo-Authoritarianism
1989–1992	Neo-Totalitarianism
1993–1997	Hard Authoritarianism
1998–2008	Soft Authoritarianism
2009–2015	Hard Authoritarianism

Figure 4.1 China's Political Orientation 1985–2015

schools of thought within the Chinese Communist Party (CCP) and its leadership: those that favor measured political liberalization managed by the Party vs. those who staunchly resist it and seek to maintain a wide variety of repressive controls over society. Let us call them the Political Reformers and the Conservatives. The first group tends to advocate broader-gauged economic reforms and believes that political loosening is necessary to facilitate economic and social development, whereas the second group does not believe that political reform necessarily needs to accompany socioeconomic reforms. The second group is also conflicted over the extent to which the economy should be "marketized"—some are proponents of measured marketization while others are advocates of a strong role for the state in the economy.

This fundamental cleavage has been evident for more than thirty years. These two tendencies are also known as "opinion groups" among scholars of Leninist single-party systems.[1] The century-long history of communist party-states reveals that these political systems are not monolithic (except perhaps North Korea or the Soviet Union during the Stalinist period) and that rather robust debates take place within the Party and intellectual classes. Scrutiny of these inner-Party debates is known as "tendency analysis."[2] Interest groups also form around corporatist economic and institutional interests.[3] Ever since the Khrushchev era in the Soviet Union (1953–1964), there have been advocates of political reform and opening in virtually all communist party-states, including China. They rise at certain intervals and then they encounter resistance from the conservative wing of the Party and are usually beaten back. They may retreat into remission and remain silent for fear of persecution, but their more liberal tendencies none-theless percolate within the Party and society until such time as a new Party leader signals that political experimentalism is again in vogue.

This, generally speaking, has been the pattern within the CCP during the post-1978 reform era as well. To be sure, even the Political Reformers believe in maintaining single-party rule and political hegemony—but they believe that the Party can be better run and can enjoy greater support from society if it is more open and tolerant. The Conservatives see this as a recipe for the Party's demise and a basic threat to the "dictatorship of the proletariat." The Conservatives want to make the Party strong too, but in their view strength only lies in assert-ing control rather than loosening it.

This tension in viewpoints has been at the core of China's political oscillations since the late 1950s, when the liberal Hundred Flowers movement triggered the repressive Anti-Rightist campaign and mass mobilization of the Great Leap Forward. That draconian period, in which upwards of 40 million died and hundreds of thousands were labeled as "rightists," gave way to a three-year thaw between 1962 and 1965 when Deng Xiaoping and other reformers took control while Mao Zedong withdrew from active rule. They instituted a wide range of economic reforms (which were the precursors to the post-1978 reforms) and loosened controls on the intelligentsia. Upon his return, Mao reacted vehemently and violently to Deng's liberal reforms by denouncing them as "revisionist" and launching the decade-long disastrous Great Proletarian Cultural Revolution. During these ten years China first convulsed in anarchy and civil war before the military intervened to restore order in 1969, after which the country sank into another round of totalitarian despotism during Mao's final years and the rule of the Gang of Four. After Mao's death in 1976 China passed through a six-year period known as the "Hua Guofeng Interregnum" (Mao's designated successor), a period of factional maneuvering between Hua and Deng Xiaoping and other elder leaders who returned to power and launched a barrage of reforms beginning in 1978.

Liberal Neo-Authoritarianism

These reforms included reconstructing the political system that had been decimated by the Cultural Revolution. Deng personally put political reform on the national agenda in 1980 with his speech "On the Reform of the System of Party and State Leadership."[4] This speech was indicative of Deng's primary priority—strengthening the *institutions* of the party-state. Yet Deng also knew that there were normative and procedural dimensions of the political system that had to be changed. He began to open up the system through a number of measures. I was a student in China at the time and witnessed the society awakening from its long socialist slumber and nightmare of the Cultural Revolution during the early years of Deng's reforms. But I also witnessed the conservative backlash during the 1984 Anti-Spiritual Pollution campaign and 1987 Anti-Bourgeois Liberalization campaign.

Deng first reached out to the intellectual class (which had known nothing but harsh repression throughout most of the Maoist era) for their support and participation in the economic reform process. He knew China had no chance of modernizing without the help of this beleaguered group of scientists and technicians. Even humanists and social scientists were no longer stigmatized, as their rightist labels were removed by decree in 1979 and they were permitted to return to work (after losing twenty-two of the most productive years of their lives!). Second, Deng established a more consultative style of decision-making whereby leading officials could draw on a range of advice provided by newly established research institutes ("think tanks").[5] No longer would policy be made by dictatorial fiat, as had been the case under Mao, which Deng blamed for China's backwardness and the chaos of the Cultural Revolution. Henceforth policymaking should, in Deng's memorable words, "seek truth from facts" (实事求是).

This latter reform led directly to the heyday of political reform in communist China, the mid- to late 1980s. Patriarchal leader Deng gave the green light to his protégés Hu Yaobang and Zhao Ziyang to explore "political structure reform" (政治体制改革). This sparked a wide range of political experiments, including the policy of "separating the Party from government" (党政分开). After Hu Yaobang was scapegoated and removed from his position as General Secretary of the CCP following a series of student-inspired "pro-democracy" demonstrations in 1986, which conservative hardliners blamed on Hu's liberalism, Zhao replaced him as Party General Secretary and continued to press for more and more political changes. Zhao was a radical reformer at heart,[6] and he drew on the advice of a number of advisors who were enamored with the theory of "neo-authoritarianism" then popular in Singapore and other Southeast Asian states. They believed that the Singaporean model could be replicated to a large degree in China, and that it would help facilitate the broad policy of "reform and opening" (改革与开放). Deng began dispatching study teams to Singapore to investigate how the city-state functioned. As scholar Bruce Gilley describes it, "Singapore's ruling People's Action Party was a model for emulation—a ruling party that tolerated symbolic opposition, promoted a market economy, and ruled by legal edicts enforced by pliant courts."[7] Governance is in the hands of educated elitist technocrats and a clean civil service. While certain elements of the Singaporean package were experimented with, Zhao and his colleagues never got a full opportunity to implement their political vision—because of the eruption of enormous "pro-democracy" demonstrations in Tiananmen Square and across China during April and May of 1989. The Beijing demonstrations were, of course, brutally suppressed on June 4, 1989. Zhao was purged and spent the remainder of his life under house arrest until he died in 2005. The events of 1989 also killed the liberal approach to political reform in China.

Neo-Totalitarianism

The crackdown was succeeded by a harsh reversion to totalitarian rule, which lasted from 1989 through 1992. Many of the harsh repressive methods that had characterized the height of totalitarianism during the Maoist era were revitalized. Hardline Stalinist-style leaders seized the instruments of power in Beijing and the military ensured their control throughout the country.

But beginning in late 1992 the situation began to change, and the draconian controls began to be relaxed. The catalyst was Deng Xiaoping's final political act—his so-called southern sojourn (南巡). In February 1992 Deng was uncomfortable with the lack of economic reform and the despotic rule of the post-Tiananmen leadership. So he took a trip to southern Guangdong province where, despite being retired from public life and now quite frail, Deng criticized political "leftism" and argued for a relaunching of economic reforms. Deng's efforts worked and, beginning with the Fourteenth Party Congress that autumn, a new leadership took power and began to gradually return to a reformist agenda—starting with economic reforms immediately and then, beginning in 1998, with political reforms.

Hard Authoritarianism

The Fourteenth Party Congress convened in October 1992 and confirmed Jiang Zemin as Deng's full successor. Jiang was the titular leader, although he still needed several years to cement his power base. On the eve of the congress, several senior hardliners were forced into retirement at Deng's behest, including his lifelong comrade-in-arms General Yang Shangkun (who was also President of the People's Republic of China at the time). It was also the first time that Hu Jintao appeared on the Politburo Standing Committee, another of Deng's last maneuvers to arrange his long-term (until 2012) succession. A young *apparatchik* who had served in the Party's Youth League and China's western provinces, Hu had been recommended to Deng by Song Ping and other Party elders. The remaining members of the Standing Committee, though, were still tainted by Tiananmen and held very conservative outlooks. This included Premier Li Peng, internal security czar Qiao Shi, and military supremo Liu Huaqing.

Thus, although Deng had succeeded in slightly shifting the balance in the leadership and had managed to kick-start economic reforms again (triggering four straight years of double-digit GDP growth), the political atmosphere remained very constrained and harshly repressive. Jiang Zemin's power was not yet consolidated and China's leaders remained traumatized from their Party's own near-death experience and having just witnessed the disintegration and collapse of the Soviet Union and East European communist party-states. They remained convinced that had they not taken lethal action in 1989, China's

Communist Party would have gone the same way. Political reform was the furthest thing from their minds. In fact, they specifically blamed Mikhail Gorbachev's political reforms, as well as the subversive "peaceful evolution" efforts of the West, for precipitating the collapse of Soviet Communist Party rule and the USSR. This was their *initial* consensus explanation for the regime implosions of 1989–1991. Over time, however, as the CCP undertook an extraordinarily detailed series of assessments of the causes of collapse, a more nuanced and fundamentally different narrative and explanation emerged. As the assessments changed, so too did the leadership's approach to political reform.

Soft Authoritarianism and Managed Political Reform From Above

The evolving assessments of the Soviet and East European overthrows are essential for understanding China's post-1989 political evolution to this day. It is also the prism through which the CCP viewed the subsequent "color revolutions" in post-Soviet Georgia (2003), Ukraine (2005), Kyrgyzstan (2005), and Moldova (2009). Myanmar also experienced a similar uprising by monks in 2007, the so-called "saffron revolution," which led to the relaxation of military rule and initiation of democratic reforms in that country. Then from December 2010 to January 2011 Tunisia kicked off the "jasmine revolution," which subsequently spread to Egypt and Libya in North Africa, and triggered political tremors across the Middle East. More recently, Malaysia and Lebanon have experienced similar mass political uprisings.

All of these global events profoundly worried and traumatized the Chinese communist leadership. Since 1989 they have lived under the paranoia and fear of being overthrown from within and subverted from without. It is a daily part of the leadership's consciousness, and the Party undertakes regular propaganda campaigns to remind the rank and file that the Party faces "life and death threats" and to constantly be on high alert against "Western hostile forces." In 2013, for example, the General Office of the CCP Central Committee issued Document No. 9: *Communique on the Current State in the Ideological Sphere.*[8] This draconian directive specifically warned all Party committees and members nationwide to guard against seven specific "false ideological trends":

1. Promoting Western Constitutional Democracy: An attempt to undermine the current leadership and the socialism with Chinese characteristics system of governance.
2. Promoting "universal values" in an attempt to weaken the theoretical foundations of the Party's leadership.
3. Promoting civil society in an attempt to dismantle the ruling party's social foundation.
4. Promoting Neo-Liberalism, attempting to change China's basic economic system.
5. Promoting the West's idea of journalism, challenging China's principle that the media and publishing system should be subject to Party discipline.
6. Promoting historical nihilism, trying to undermine the history of the CCP and of New China.
7. Questioning the policy of Reform and Opening and the socialist nature of socialism with Chinese characteristics.

Document No. 9 ominously concluded: "The contest between infiltration and anti-infiltration efforts in the ideological sphere is as severe as ever, and so long as we persist in CCP leadership and socialism with Chinese characteristics, the position of Western anti-China forces will not change, and they will continue to point the spearhead of Westernizing, splitting, and color revolutions at China. In the face of these threats, we must not let down our guard or decrease our vigilance."[9]

Understanding these genuine twin fears of internal opposition and external subversion is absolutely fundamental to contextualizing what the CCP leadership has done in the political sphere over the last twenty-five years. While the fear has been constant, the internal assessments within the Party evolved over time from 1989 until 2004 (when an official conclusion was given at the Fourth Plenum of the Sixteenth Party Congress). I have detailed this evolution in my previous book *China's Communist Party: Atrophy and Adaptation*.[10] Essentially there were two main competing interpretations within the CCP.

The first group were the Conservatives: those who believed that the proto-liberal reforms of Gorbachev worked in tandem with the subversive "peaceful evolution" tactics of the West to directly precipitate the collapse of the Soviet Union and sow the seeds of "counter-revolution" elsewhere. They similarly concluded that the compromises made by the ruling regimes with protestors in East Germany, Poland, and Czechoslovakia contributed directly to their downfalls—whereas if force had been used, as in Beijing in 1989, they could have likely survived. When the Ceauşescu regime in Romania decided to use force in Timisoara in December 1989 the military and state security services split and abandoned the regime, with the result that Nicolae Ceauşescu and his wife Elena were overthrown and executed on Christmas Eve. We now know the same occurred in Leipzig on October 9, 1989, signaling the end of the East German regime, as the communist leadership opted for the "Chinese solution." On that evening Stasi forces were armed and instructed to use lethal force, but they demurred when confronted by massive demonstrations far larger than they antici-pated.[11] Unlike Beijing, where regular army units were called in, the paramilitary Stasi was not equipped or prepared to undertake a large-scale lethal suppression.

From these events, the CCP Conservatives drew three principal conclusions:

- Do not engage in proto-liberal reforms within the Party or gov-ernment, and maintain absolute dominance of, and resolute control over, the party-state apparatus.
- Anticipate unrelenting efforts from the West (particularly the United States) to undermine and subvert the regime from within—the so-called policy of "peaceful evolution" (和平演变), to peacefully evolve communist systems into democratic systems. In particular, be on high alert against the development of civil society and religious actors—which are sub-versive in their own right, but will receive support from Western governments, intelligence agencies, and NGOs.
- Strengthen and maintain absolute control by the Communist Party over the internal security services and military, and resist dangerous attempts to "nationalize" them.

These were—and still are—the central lessons learned by the Conservatives in the Chinese Communist Party. In addition, they concluded that growing the economy and being integrated into the inter-national system were further guarantors necessary for survival (both of which the Soviet and East European regimes lacked). The Conservatives implemented these consensus measures between 1989 and 1998.

However, over time, a second line of analysis emerged within the CCP, giving rise to a second group—advocates of proactive and managed political reform. Beginning in the mid-1990s, CCP analysts began to dig deeper into the causes of collapse of the USSR and the individual cases in Eastern Europe. As they did so they discovered that the easy and convenient explanations offered by the Conservatives were not the entire story. They agreed with the Conservatives that splits in the security apparatus at critical moments produced the ultimate unraveling of those regimes. They also agreed that economic growth and integration into the world order were essential elements that could likely have helped sustain the regimes' grip on power. And they were aware of the "peaceful evolution" efforts of the West. But the Political Reformers broke with the Conservatives over the issue of Gorbachev's *glasnost* and *perestroika*. They did not necessarily agree with all of his policies, but they concluded that the Soviet party-state was in dire need of reformation. The essence of their critique of the causes of Soviet collapse had to do with the decades-long atrophy of the Party apparatus itself.[12] In their revisionist view, the Soviet Union actually began to decline under Stalin in the 1930s! With the exception of Nikita Khrushchev's reforms from 1956 to 1964 (when he was ousted from power), this line of Chinese analysis concluded that the USSR had experienced an inexorable six-decade-long decline—during which the party-state became sclerotic, ossified, top-heavy, elitist, overly bureaucratic, and corrupt, while the country's economy had become militarized during the Cold War, and Moscow's foreign policy had become adventurist, revisionist, chauvinistic, hegemonic, and "social imperialist."

The upshot of their analysis was that by the time Gorbachev came to power and launched his reforms, the economic and political systems were already too badly broken and thus unable to withstand his shock therapy. To be sure, they did not agree with all of Gorbachev's reforms, but they drew the principal conclusion that for a ruling communist party to stay alive it was imperative to be proactive and dynamic. Stasis was a recipe for sclerosis, atrophy, decline, and ultimate collapse. These Chinese analysts perceived many of the same processes to have precipitated the institutional crises that gripped the East European party-states (in addition to the important fact that they had not had their own indigenous revolutions; their regimes had been imposed externally by the Soviets).

Thus in the decade after 1989 the CCP's internal assessments evolved and two distinct cohorts emerged—those who favored managed political opening from above, and those who resisted it. The Conservatives prevailed until around 1997, when the leadership balance had shifted at the Fifteenth Party Congress.[13] After that Congress, Li Peng, the reviled Premier and public face of the Tiananmen massacre, was finally shunted aside to a ceremonial position at the National People's Congress. He was replaced as Premier by the dynamic, decisive, get-things-done Zhu Rongji. Zhu took immediate charge and oversaw five years of systematic overhaul of the nation's economic structure. Hu Jintao was also elevated to the Politburo Standing Committee. The remaining Tiananmen hardliners went into retirement, and other senior leaders were reshuffled. It was in this changed leadership context that Jiang Zemin devoted a whole section of his speech to the Congress to political reforms, declaring that "we should press ahead with the reform of the political structure."[14] It subtly signaled that the Political Reformers had reasserted themselves—thus kicking off a ten-year period of efforts to manage political change from above.

During this period, which began during the last four years of Jiang Zemin's tenure and continued under the first six of Hu Jintao, the Political Reformers stealthily but steadily experimented with loosening a variety of political controls in several spheres. During this decade the Party:

- experimented with voting for multicandidate Party secretaries, while expanding nationwide multicandidate elections for local government officials;
- recruited more businesspeople and intellectuals into the Party (Jiang Zemin's theory of the "Three Represents");
- expanded party consultation with non-Party groups—so-called "consultative democracy" (协商民主) and "multi-party cooperation" (多党合作);
- increased the transparency of the Politburo's proceedings;
- improved discussion and feedback mechanisms within the Party—so-called "inner-Party democracy"(党内民主);
- regularized consultations between the CCP and Chinese People's Political Consultative Congress (政协);
- rebuilt local Party cells and committees;
- implemented more meritocratic criteria for evaluation and promotions for all cadres (by the CCP Organization Department and State Council Ministry of Personnel);
- instituted a system of mandatory mid-career training for all 45 million state and Party cadres (three months every three years);
- enforced term limits and retirement requirements;
- rotated officials and military officers between job assignments every couple of years;
- loosened controls on the state and private media;
- gave intellectuals greater scope and license to create and voice more pluralistic opinions;
- allowed the dramatic growth of civil society, including domestic and foreign NGOs;
- introduced more foreign ideas in the higher educational system.

Through these reforms the Party leadership was clearly trying to incrementally liberalize and loosen the political system (from above) without losing control of the process. This managed approach grew directly out of the Political Reformers' alternative interpretation of the causes of collapse of the former communist party-states. They believed that *proactive change* was the only way to avoid the trap of stagnancy that afflicted all of those former regimes. This view prevailed inside the CCP until 2009, and became known as the "resilient authoritarian" or "adaptation" paradigm among many foreign China specialists.[15]

Up until the about-face in 2009, the political reformers were dominant during the last years of Jiang Zemin's and early years of Hu Jintao's rule. One important commonality that Jiang Zemin and Hu Jintao shared was another senior leader named Zeng Qinghong (Figure 4.2).

In my view, Zeng was the main mastermind behind the Political Reformers' efforts.[16] Zeng was Jiang's closest confidant whom he brought with him from Shanghai (one of the so-called "Shanghai Gang"). Once at the Center, Zeng consolidated his own power base quickly as his positions and influence progressively expanded. After chairing the powerful Party Politburo Secretariat, he went on to head the CCP's Organization Department and the Central Party School, before capping his career as Vice-President of the People's Republic. Throughout this time Zeng was a senior member of the Politburo Standing Committee and Jiang Zemin's right-hand man.

While known as a shrewd inside operator who was fiercely loyal to Jiang, Zeng also evinced relatively progressive views of politics and the role of the Communist Party. This became clear at the Fourth Plenum of the Sixteenth Central Committee in 2004, when the Party issued a major *Decision on the Enhancement of the Party's Governing Capacity*. Party leader Hu Jintao put Zeng Qinghong in charge of the

Figure 4.2 Zeng Qinghong
Source: Reuters.

drafting committee for the *Decision*. The document was a culmination of the CCP's years of assessment of the causes of collapse of the
former Soviet Union and its implications for the CCP. As the *Decision*
noted: "We must develop a stronger sense of crisis, draw experience
and lessons from the success and failure of other ruling parties in the
world, and enhance our governance capability in a more earnest and
conscientious manner. . . . Vigorously enhancing the Party's governing
capabilities is a major strategic subject with a bearing on the future and
destiny of the Chinese nation, the life and death of the Party, as well as
the lasting stability and prosperity of the country."[17]

Zeng Qinghong also gave the key speech at the conclusion of the Plenum interpreting the document and summing up the lessons of the Soviet implosion—it was a blueprint and mandate for managed political change from above.[18] Zeng blamed the Soviet collapse on *stasis* (among other things): "A Party that is not dynamic and does not change with the times (跟上时代潮流与时俱进) will become moribund and cut off from its popular base until it ultimately dies. The Communist Party in the Soviet Union was a big party with an 88-year history and 15 million members, yet it was disbanded. Communist parties in the Soviet Union and Eastern Europe lost their status as parties in power. Although many factors were involved, one important reason was that in their long time in power their system of governing became rigid, their ability to govern declined, people were dissatisfied with what the local officials accomplished while in charge, and they became seriously isolated from the masses of people."[19] By the time Zeng gave the speech in 2004, he was in fact already six years into implementing his political reform program. The program continued for another four years before the Party sharply pivoted away from it during the second half of 2009.[20] The fact that Zeng had to officially retire after the National People's Congress in 2008 meant that the political reform program now lacked its principal mastermind and top-level benefactor.

With Zeng's retirement the only remaining senior leader in favor of political reform was Premier Wen Jiabao. During Wen's final years in office (he retired in 2012), he gave several speeches and interviews calling for enhanced political reform and openness. In one interview with CNN in 2010 (which was not circulated inside China) Wen said: "I and all the Chinese people have such conviction that China will make continuous progress and the people's wishes and need for democracy and freedom are irresistible. I hope you will be able to gradually see the continuous progress of China. In spite of some resistance I will advance within the realm of my capabilities political restructuring."[21] Two years later Wen described political reform as an "urgent task."[22] In his swan song at the 2012 National People's Congress, Wen opined again that political reform was direly needed lest "China experience another historical tragedy like the Cultural Revolution."[23] Wen's brave voice was the lone one in the senior leadership during 2009–2012. After he retired, there have been no top-level advocates and those within the party-state system or society have kept silent for fear of punishment.

Retrenchment and a Return to Hard Authoritarianism

It is difficult to put an exact date on it, but throughout the year of 2009 the CCP leadership retrenched and reverted to the Conservatives, completely abandoning the Political Reformers' agenda described above (with the exception of term limits, retirement regulations, and mid-career cadre training). No formal announcement was made, but the atmosphere unmistakably shifted during the second half of that year. I was living in Beijing on sabbatical at the time and witnessed the changes. Although the CCP endorsed another very progressive *Decision* at its Fourth Plenum in September 2009, it was a stillborn document. The contents had already been overtaken by events and had died a quiet death before the *Decision* was published. The document reiterated many of the political reforms of the previous decade, and suggested that Zeng's political reforms would continue. But it was not to be. Discussions I had with Party members at the time indicated that the document had been one year in preparation, had passed through multiple drafts, and was seen as a kind of culmination statement of the reforms in the political arena over the previous decade (official Chinese documents are frequently this way, summarizing policies that have already been undertaken rather than announcing new initiatives). Moreover, fourth plenums traditionally deal with politics, so the regime had to address the topic and issue a concluding communiqué. Although abandoned afterwards, this *Decision* (like the one issued at the Fourth Plenum in 2004) could very well form the basis for a *return* to the Party's political reform agenda, should the composition and disposition of the leadership change again.

A series of events during 2008–2009 contributed to the Party's increased nervousness and political about-face. In March 2008 Lhasa, Tibet, erupted in riots. This was repeated in Urumqi, Xinjiang, during the summer of 2009. The 2008 Olympics and the preparations for the massive military parade in Beijing to commemorate the sixty-fifth anniversary of the People's Republic of China on October 1 (both of which I witnessed) also offered the regime a golden opportunity to test its security procedures and erect a tight security dragnet over the capital city. The rising number of incidents of mass unrest across the country had also catalyzed a growing sub-provincial security apparatus.

Personnel and bureaucratic considerations were also important, I believe. Zeng Qinghong had retired and there was no senior patron of the political reform program. Hu Jintao was not a strong leader and did not wield a great deal of authority within the Party or military (he commanded respect only by virtue of his official position). His *apparatchik* background probably predisposed him against the political reform agenda (although it had been implemented under his aegis during the previous six years). Hu was, I would argue, easily manipulated by more powerful figures and institutional interests. Around that time four powerful bureaucracies that had a strong stake in tightening state control coalesced into a powerful coalition: the Party propaganda apparatus, internal security organs (Ministries of State and Public Security), the state-owned enterprise sector, and military and paramilitary (People's Liberation Army and People's Armed Police) forces. These four powerful bureaucracies (which I label the "Iron Quadrangle") and the Politburo members that headed them (including now-disgraced and imprisoned Zhou Yongkang) were in a position to persuade the pliable Hu Jintao (who was no longer subject to Zeng Qinghong's active role in the Politburo) that political liberalization from above would cascade out of control and endanger Party rule. Instead, they made the case for abandoning the political reform program, reversing the main elements of it, and instituting tight security and Party controls in its place.[24] These bureaucracies also stood to financially benefit from a political tightening-up, as there is Big Money in repression. The internal security budget topped the military budget for the first time in 2011 ($83.5 billion vs. $81.2 billion) and did so for the three subsequent fiscal years. Finally, the global financial crisis imbued the Chinese leadership with a sense of hubris over the decline of the Washington Consensus and seeming vindication of the Beijing Consensus models of development. Taken together, I believe these factors all contributed to Beijing's political pivot in 2009.

Since Xi Jinping came to power at the Eighteenth CCP Congress in November 2012, the reign of the Conservatives has continued. Xi has proven to be a very anti-liberal leader and he has overseen an even greater intensification of the repression evident since 2009. There has been an unremitting crackdown on all forms of dissent and social activists; the internet and social media have been subjected to much tighter controls (see chapter 3); Christian crosses and churches are being demolished; Uighurs and Tibetans have been subject to ever-greater persecution; hundreds of rights lawyers have been detained and put on trial; public gatherings are restricted; a wide range of publications are censored; foreign textbooks have been officially banned from university classrooms; intellectuals are under tight scrutiny; foreign and domestic NGOs have been subjected to unprecedented governmental

Figure 4.3 Xi Jinping
Source: Flickr.com.

regulatory pressures and many have been forced to leave China; attacks on "foreign hostile forces" occur with regularity; and the "stability maintenance" security *apparatchiks* have blanketed the country. A swath of intrusive new regulations and laws concerning national security, cyber security, terrorism, and nongovernmental organizations have been drafted and enacted. China is today more repressive than at any time since the post-Tiananmen 1989–1992 period.[25]

To be certain, Xi Jinping (Figure 4.3) is a genuinely tough ruler and strong leader—just what many believe China needed after the "eight lost years" of drift under his predecessor Hu Jintao.[26] Xi exudes self-conviction and personal confidence. The recently deceased Singaporean statesman Lee Kuan Yew said of Xi: "He has iron in his soul, more than Hu Jintao, who ascended the ranks without experiencing the trials and tribulations that Xi endured."[27]

In a relatively short period of time Xi has amassed greater personal power than any Chinese leader since Deng Xiaoping (some believe since Mao) and he has centralized and concentrated institutional power of the Party, state, and military in his own hands. He has encouraged a personality cult to be built up around him. He is a proactive leader, is extremely active in the domestic and international arenas, and he has articulated a clear and detailed vision for China at home and abroad. Many of his views are set forth in *The Governance of China*, an expansive 515-page volume of Xi's collected speeches reminiscent of the *Selected Works of Chairman Mao*.[28] Not long after assuming office Xi enunciated his "Chinese Dream"—a vision for "the great rejuvenation of the Chinese nation." Xi oversaw the drafting of the Third Plenum package of economic reforms (see chapter 2). Since coming to power, Xi has sought to strengthen the Party's power across the board, stripping away the limited autonomy previously granted to other institutional actors and reasserting CCP controls over a wide range of institutions and activities.[29]

Perhaps most significantly, Xi has unleashed an unprecedented campaign against corruption throughout the Party, government, military, and state security bureaucracies. So far the campaign is proceeding with vigor. Large numbers of ministerial-level, provincial-level, and local-level officials have been investigated and punished: altogether during 2013–2014 over 180,000 CCP members and government officials, 74 provincial-level officials, 4,024 PLA officers (including 82 generals), and 68 ministerial and vice-ministerial level officials.[30] High-level Party and military leaders (so-called "tigers") have been brought down and incarcerated: Bo Xilai, Zhou Yongkang, Xu Caihou, Guo Buoxiong, Ling Jihua, and others. The campaign continues, is very popular with the public, and is undoubtedly a good thing for China (but it also reveals the pervasiveness of the problem). On the other hand, the campaign is turning out to be a selective purge. Many members of Jiang Zemin's factional network, and a rising number of Hu Jintao's, have been brought down—yet none of Xi's own princeling associates have been touched. In a political system that very much has patron-client networks at its core, it would not seem particularly astute to purge the networks of Xi's two predecessors while they are still alive; co-opting them would seem a better strategy. The campaign has also had the corollary side effect of paralyzing the cadre system across the country, as all 45 million Party and state cadres (as well as thousands of military officers) go from day to day wondering if they will be the next to be caught in Xi's trap. In other words, while necessary and welcome, the anti-corruption campaign is seriously stressing the system that has very much come to depend on it. Moreover, the campaign is targeting the behavioral *manifestations* of corruption (bribery, private villas, lavish lifestyles, luxury goods, mistresses)—not the systemic *sources* of corruption (lack of transparency, lack of autonomous media, lack of autonomous judiciary, rent-seeking, slack auditing and tax systems, and lack of political competition).

But Xi's hard personality and assertive policies belie a Party and political system that is extremely fragile on the inside, in my view. Chinese use the proverb *waiying, neiruan* (外硬内软)—hard on the outside, soft on the inside—which is a fitting description of the condition of the Chinese communist regime today. The regime's repression is symptomatic of its deep and profound *insecurity*. This is not a secure and confident regime; quite the contrary. Confident and secure regimes do not need to rule by repression. The sense of political vulnerability is palpable. China's leaders face the litany of serious domestic social and economic problems detailed in the previous two chapters, as well as a growing range of external challenges examined in the next chapter. They have good reasons to be fearful.

There is a theory circulating in China-watching circles that Xi's harsh tactics presage a more open and reformist direction later in his term. I do not buy the argument, just as I was dubious of the argument when Xi came to power in 2012 that he was a Political Reformer who would open up the system.[31] If liberalization were to occur, it would be forced on him by a coalition of other Politburo figures—and this is not inconceivable following the Nineteenth Party Congress in 2017. But my sense of Xi as a leader and the current regime is that they view politics in zero-sum terms: sharing power and empowering other civic actors in the system, in their view, are sure steps towards the demise of the system and their personal loss of power and privileges. Xi and the current CCP leadership are very much in the Conservative tradition described above. It is probably no accident that Xi Jinping's "vision volume" of speeches (*The Governance of China*, noted above) contains sections on virtually all areas of public policy confronting China—economic development, culture, science and technology, ecology, law, corruption, society, national defense, foreign relations, and others—but has no section on politics or political reform. It is a book theoretically about governance but with no discussion of politics—very odd, but very revealing. All of Xi's predecessors dating back to Deng Xiaoping have spoken about the need for political reform, but not him. It does not seem to be part of his vocabulary or consciousness.

It is true that Xi has emphasized the "rule of law," and the Fourth Plenum of the Eighteenth Central Committee was devoted entirely to the subject (recall that the fourth plenums of the Sixteenth and Seventeenth Central Committees, before Xi came to power, were devoted to political reform and "Party building"), but for Xi law seems to be a tool in the hands of the party-state to enforce its writ and rule. The Fourth Plenum produced an important *Resolution on Certain Major Issues Concerning Comprehensively Advancing the Law-Based Governance of China*.[32] Throughout the document it is made explicitly clear that the Party shall guide the application of law; for example, "The Party's leadership is the most essential feature of socialism with Chinese characteristics and the most fundamental guarantee for socialist rule of law in China. The need to exercise the Party's leadership throughout the whole process and in every respect of law-based governance of the country is a basic lesson we have learned in developing socialist rule of law in China."[33] The Party itself is regulated by its own set of regulations (党内法规) and institutions such as the Central Discipline Inspection Commission (中央纪律检查委员会). If Party officials are also found to have violated state laws, they are then turned over for prosecution by the state legal system. As veteran China legal scholar Stanley Lubman observes,[34] the Party may well understand the need for judiciary proceedings to be more autonomous of Party dictates, but because the Party casts such a wide net in its definition of seditious or politically sensitive activities it limits any real separation of legal institutions from the Party. After all, it is not by accident that the CCP oversees what it calls the "political-legal system" (政法系统). Nonetheless, some legal scholars see kernels of potential progress in the Fourth Plenum *Decision*. As Donald Clarke notes, "The *Decision* denounces attempts by leading officials to interfere with court cases and calls for the establishment of a system to keep track of such attempts."[35] Clarke also notes that the *Decision* also embraces the principle of the presumption of innocence (疑罪从无) and an enhanced role for "people's assessors" (pseudo-juries) to hear cases in tandem with tribunals of judges.[36]

Xi Jinping is supposed to remain in power until 2022, when he is (by constitutional provision) supposed to retire at the age of sixty-nine after serving two five-year terms in office as President. This carefully choreographed script will likely play out as planned. However, there are two possibilities that could disrupt the design.

The first is the chance that Xi is overthrown before then. While unlikely, it is not entirely out of the realm of the conceivable. Xi has alienated a very large number of senior and middle-ranking cadres through his anti-corruption campaign and his personal amalgamation of power.[37] The purges in the military (more than 4,000 officers and 82 generals, including two former high-ranking Central Military Commission members) have been more sweeping than at any time in PRC history, including in the wake of the Lin Biao affair of 1971. Xi needs the support of the military brass as well as the rank-and-file in the People's Liberation Army—it is thus very surprising, and highly risky, to be purging the PLA. Chinese communist politics have a very long history of military involvement in elite politics, and senior officers have intervened to overthrow and arrest civilian Party leaders on more than one occasion in the past. When this has occurred in the past it has been done in conjunction with disgruntled senior civilian Politburo-level leaders. While hard evidence is scant, it is safe to assume that Xi's purges of former high-ranking leaders Bo Xilai, Zhou Yongkang, and Ling Jihua (not to mention thousands of second-tier but high-ranking officials linked to senior sitting leaders) has ruffled more than a few feathers in the Zhongnanhai. The Hong Kong media (often a source of leaked but accurate information on elite maneuverings) have been filled with stories that Jiang Zemin has warned Xi to back off and tamp down the anti-corruption campaign. A large number of Jiang's protégés have already been arrested. Perhaps most risky for Xi are the persistent rumors since 2014 that none other than Zeng Qinghong is the next "tiger" in his sights. Given Zeng's previous high-level positions and closeness to Jiang, and central role in the 1998–2008 political reforms described above, this would be an unprecedented and highly risky move on Xi's part. It could trigger a coup against him (Zeng also has his own ties to the military). In what is perhaps a sign that he is concerned about such a possibility, Xi has replaced his personal bodyguard unit twice in the past year.

The second possibility that would disrupt the expectation that Xi will step down in 2022 is that he might maneuver to extend his stay in office. By that time, he may be so powerful, the hypothesis goes, that he would stay on in some official capacity—perhaps resurrecting the position of Chairman of the Party (as Jiang Zemin attempted to do when he similarly did not wish to let go of power in 2002). Even if he did retire as intended, at sixty-nine, he would become the behind-the-scenes godfather of Chinese politics for a very long time to come.

Pathways to China's Political Future

Given this background and the current situation, where do Chinese politics go from here? What can be anticipated and what alternative possibilities exist for the future of China's polity?

As we saw with respect to the economy and society in chapters 2 and 3, China's leaders have essentially two basic choices when it comes to politics. They can either continue with the Hard Authoritarian policies of control and repression pursued since 2009—in which case all of the economic and social problems and bottlenecks described in the previous two chapters will continue to fester and worsen—or they can return to the Soft Authoritarian politically reformist policies pursued from 1998 to 2008, which would involve a significant loosening and liberalization of the political system while facilitating progress in addressing many (but not all) of the economic and social challenges.

There are also two other possibilities, both of which are matters of degree greater than the two just noted. The first would be even *greater* repression and attempted reconstruction of a totalitarian state with significantly strengthened controls over all facets of civic life. It is conceivable that things could get worse—much worse—than the current situation.

Alternatively, the regime could conceivably go in the opposite direction, well *beyond* the managed political reforms of the 1998–2008 period—essentially creating a semi-democratic polity similar to Singapore where multiple parties compete but a single party remains dominant. There are many other elements of this model (described below), but only with this kind of radical reform and restructuring will China be able to realize its full creative potential to become an innovative society and dynamic nation.

Thus, as in previous chapters, I envision four alternative future pathways for China's polity:[38] Hard Authoritarianism, Neo-Totalitarianism, Soft Authoritarianism, and Semi-Democracy. The first is the current situation, the second would be a significant step backward, the third has been tried before and could be embraced again, and the fourth would be a bold step forward for China. Let us consider each of these possibilities in turn.

Continuation of the Status Quo: Hard Authoritarianism

It is certainly conceivable that the regime can continue with its current Hard Authoritarian repressive policies. Seven years of these policies is already a long time, and Xi Jinping and the party-state show no signs of changing course. To the contrary, they are "doubling down" and ramping up controls and repression across the country.

However, I would argue that the current (post-2009) situation of tightened controls and increased repression only accentuates and makes more acute the already severe tensions within society and between the party-state and society. In my view, such Hard Authoritarianism only serves to *accelerate* the Party's existing atrophy and decline. Tightened control reflects a zero-sum approach to power and a highly insecure regime that lacks intrinsic confidence and does not trust its own population. Repression reflects weakness, not strength.

When considering the Party's weakness it is also useful to view it through a comparative lens—in fact, through two sets of lenses.

The first is to compare the CCP with other authoritarian newly industrializing countries. There has not been a single case of such an authoritarian country successfully transitioning through the Middle Income Trap and not simultaneously adopting a democratic political system. Most of those that failed to make the transition remain authoritarian. So there is a very clear correlation between economic openness and political openness, as symbolized in the J-Curve discussed in chapter 2. A continuation of Hard Authoritarian policies fails to contribute the conditions for advancing the envisioned Third Plenum economic reforms, thus contributing to the continuing stagnation of the economy and China bogging down indefinitely in the Middle Income Trap. Such policies will also make more acute the social problems the regime faces.

The second is to compare the CCP with other Leninist parties. Leninist party-states have a distinct set of characteristics that set them apart from other authoritarian systems. They are generally much more institutionalized and organized, with the Leninist party penetrating and dominating all aspects of government, military, and society. Leninist systems are like huge machines, with a vast number of intricate cogs that make them function—while many other authoritarian regimes are patriarchal and personalistic, with a single dictator, low levels of institutionalization of the party-state apparatus, and heavily reliant on a military loyal to the leader to sustain the system in power.

Leninist systems, which have been carefully studied by political scientists for decades during and after the Cold War, also pass through identifiable and predictable stages of development, a kind of political life cycle: revolution and seizure of power → consolidation of power and imposition of totalitarian controls → bureaucratization and mobilization → hard authoritarianism and bureaucratic atrophy → soft authoritarianism, adaptation, and pluralism.[39] China very much followed this progression, transitioning to this final stage of political development from 1998 to 2008. The Soviet Union tried to make this transition under Gorbachev, but the atrophy of the previous stage was already so fully progressed that the system could not absorb the reforms and thus collapsed. The same was true of the East European communist party-states. China, however, was moving along this path of adaption (with the exception of the 1989–1998 post-Tiananmen retrenchment), until it halted the pluralistic adaption and managed political opening in 2009 and reverted to Hard Authoritarianism and reassertion of controls by the party-state. There is not a single example of a Leninist party-state successfully adapting for a prolonged period of time. They have all collapsed, with one exception (albeit non-communist): Taiwan under the Kuomintang, when in 1986 President Chiang Ching-kuo began the protracted process of successfully making the transition from a reforming and adaptive Leninist party-state to a fully democratic system. In other words, there is a precedent—a *Chinese* precedent—for Soft Authoritarian Leninist regimes peacefully transitioning to a democratic system. China was following this path of adaptive opening with managed political opening from above prior to 2009, although there was no intention to transition to a democracy. It was a gamble that the CCP leadership was making during 1998–2008, and it is a gamble that they could return to in the future, but in 2009 they decided it was not a gamble worth taking. Hence the repressive retrenchment to Hard Authoritarianism.

This reversion toward increased coercion, control, and bureaucratization has been coupled with two other telltale signs of Leninist regime atrophy. The first is the apparent feigned compliance with the regime's propaganda. The Chinese communist regime spews out propaganda slogan after slogan day after day—yet cadres and citizens alike go through the transparently false motions of pretended adherence. When visiting China one quickly realizes that even Party loyalists are just going through the motions. It is hard to miss the theater of pretense that has permeated the Chinese body politic for the past few years. Chinese politics always exhibits a theatrical veneer where official rhetoric and events are staged. Party members, officials, and citizens alike know they should conform to these rituals by participating in such meetings and parroting back official slogans. This behavior is known in Chinese as the act of *biaotai*, "to declare where one stands." Party members and citizens simply go through the motions of repeating the latest slogan verbatim (if they can remember it) in front of their colleagues. This false behavior and feigned compliance has become increasingly apparent in China in recent years—the regime's propaganda has lost its power, and the emperor has no clothes. No one believes the leaders' edicts anymore; they just parrot them. When this occurs, as it did in the Soviet Union and Eastern Europe, it is a key indicator that the regime lacks normative support even among its own members.

The second telltale sign that the regime is corroding from within (in addition to widespread corruption) is that the economic elites—who in many cases also are Party members (given the nexus of commercial cronyism)—have begun to leave the country in increasingly large numbers.[40] China's economic elite have one foot out the door, and they are ready to flee *en masse* if the system really begins to crumble. In 2014, Shanghai's Hurun Research Institute, which studies China's wealthy, found that 64 percent of "high net worth individuals" it polled—393 millionaires and billionaires—were either emigrating or planning to do so.[41] Rich Chinese are sending their children to study abroad in record numbers (in itself, an indictment of the quality of the Chinese higher education system). They are buying property abroad at record levels and prices, and are parking their financial assets overseas, often in well-shielded tax havens and shell companies. Meanwhile, Beijing is trying to extradite back to China a large number of alleged financial fugitives living abroad. When a country's elite—many of them Party members—flee in such large numbers, it is a telling sign of their lack of confidence in the regime and the nation's future.

Going forward into the future, watch for other indicators that the terminal cancer plaguing the Chinese communist body politic is metastasizing: failure of security *apparatchiks* to enforce repression; failure of internet and social media monitors to censor; defections of officials abroad; splits in the military and internal security services; elite factionalism; pushback from intellectuals; ad hoc protests; and other dissident activities.

It is for all of these reasons that I assess the Chinese Leninist system to once again be in a state of atrophy and inexorable decline. Many of these elements have also been apparent when previous Chinese dynasties waned. In short, Hard Authoritarianism is a recipe for economic stagnation, social instability, and the political decline of the Chinese Communist Party. Xi Jinping and his comrades may think this is the right path for China and for their remaining in power—but I believe it is a fundamental miscalculation.

Revived Neo-Totalitarianism

It is also conceivable that the regime might further *intensify* its repression and controls over society and try to resurrect and rebuild the totalitarian state China once was. Many of the coercive institutions and instruments of that era remain in place, while massive "stability maintenance" budgets and new surveillance technologies afford new Orwellian opportunities for the regime. Such a leftist lurch backward could be precipitated by a social, economic, or political crisis (similar to 1989); it could come about as a result of particularly hardline leaders and their coercive bureaucracies asserting themselves; or both.

The reference point for such a scenario would be 1989–1992. It would involve the following: strict state controls over all major media and social media; widespread detentions and arrests of intellectuals, students, lawyers, writers, and activists; martial law being proclaimed in Tibet and Xinjiang (perhaps elsewhere); termination of domestic and foreign NGOs; deployment of paramilitary PAP troops and stepped-up police patrols throughout Chinese cities; strict controls over foreign and internal travel for Chinese citizens; limited visas for foreigners and careful monitoring of Chinese interactions with them; xenophobic campaigns in the cultural and educational arenas; and other repressive measures. Such domestic repression could also be paired with aggressive behavior externally.

While difficult to implement, this is not a completely unfeasible scenario—particularly if a large-scale uprising or widespread social unrest occurred. Such unrest would give the regime a tailor-made excuse to crack down further. There are certainly hardline individuals in the leadership and elements of China's "coercive apparatus" that would relish such a retreat into even greater repression. The question is: would society stand for it? With 700 million citizens connected to the internet and social media such as WeChat, would they stand to have their communications cut off and shut down? Millions of Chinese now have passports—might they just leave the country under such circumstances? Would citizens go back to monitoring each other or tolerating secret police among them? One does not know the answers to these questions until the time comes—but it is no longer 1989 in China.

From "Shou" Back to "Fang"

Alternatively, the regime could move in the opposite direction: becoming more open, tolerant, and liberal. The repetitive *"fang-shou* cycle," described above, could shift again. For this to occur, the Communist Party and its leadership need to abandon their zero-sum approach to political power and realize that more liberal and open policies would far more effectively address the systemic economic and social challenges they face while simultaneously actually *prolonging* CCP rule and their power. A more positive-sum approach to political power does not necessarily require the end of one-party (CCP) rule or the advent of a full democratic system. Of course, a full democratic system—a multiparty system with separation of powers, direct elections, universal suffrage, guaranteed civil rights, free media, fully open civil society and public sphere, full market economy, and other attributes associated with real democracies—would be optimal for China to achieve its full greatness. But it is not necessary in order to untether the full creative forces in Chinese society that will power a new wave of innovative development. This can be accomplished, in my view, through either of two types of systems.

A Return to Soft Authoritarianism

The first would be a return to the Soft Authoritarian (Managed Political Reform from Above) policies that the CCP pursued during the 1998–2008 period. This would not be a new policy—it would be a *return* to the old set of policies Zeng Qinghong engineered during that decade.

There is a strong precedent for it. Moreover, there are important CCP-approved documents endorsing such a policy direction—the *Decisions* of the Fourth Plenums of the Sixteenth and Seventeenth Central Committees, to be precise. These two documents were approved at the highest levels of the Party and are systematic and programmatic blueprints for an alternative Soft Authoritarian rule, even if they were subsequently shelved.

As we saw at the beginning of this chapter, Chinese politics has oscillated between repression and reform. Each time the repressors regain control they revamp and reassert the coercive methods they used in the past. Similarly, each time the political reformers regain power they open the file drawer, blow the dust off the previously used reform plans, and say to themselves, "Now, where were we (before the most recent repressive hiatus)?" There are many, many political reformers and liberally inclined Party members throughout the CCP system and intelligentsia. I know them; I have met and have talked with them. They are not at all happy with the current direction of the country or the Party. But they have been lying low since 2009. They have no choice. But they have learned from the past that their time may come again.

One example is Yu Keping. Yu simultaneously holds the positions of Director of the Center for Chinese Governance at Peking University and Deputy Director of the Central Compilation and Translations Bureau of the Central Committee of the CCP. Yu has also been an informal advisor to the senior leadership. Among his many progressive writings was an article he published in 2006 entitled "Democracy Is a Good Thing" (民主是个好东西).[42]

If consensus again emerged in the leadership that *loosening* political controls was desirable, the reformers could again return to the file drawer, dust off the Sixteenth and Seventeenth Central Committee Fourth Plenum *Decisions*, approved by their predecessors, and they would have a ready-made blueprint for political relaxation and managed reform from above (just as Deng did after the Cultural Revolution). This is entirely feasible *if* there were liberally inclined leaders in the majority at the top of the system—which there are not today. It will require a fairly large-scale change in the composition of the CCP elite. This could come at the Nineteenth Party Congress in 2017. At that time, four of the seven members of the current Politburo Standing Committee and thirteen of twenty-five Politburo members are due to retire (because of age requirements). This would open the door to a political reform faction to return to power. Nine of the twelve Politburo members who will remain in office have politically reformist records— most notably Li Keqiang, Wang Huning, Li Yuanchao, Wang Yang, Liu Qibao, Sun Zhengcai, and Hu Chunhua. This is a potentially powerful coalition at the pinnacle of Party power. Even if Xi Jinping disagreed with an opening to political reform again, this coalition could be powerful enough to push it through. If Xi tried to block it, a stalemate and showdown could well occur—and Xi would either have his hand forced or he might well be removed from power.

Such a return to a politically more liberal agenda would do much to address the bottlenecks holding back the bold economic and social reforms China so badly needs, some of which are embodied in the Third Plenum documents. Such a political loosening, while welcome, would not, however, be a panacea. First of all, by 2017 the reforms will have been stalled for eight years—during which time the problems they are meant to address have become far more acute. Moreover, as during the 1998–2008 period, there is no guarantee that managed political opening from above could be accomplished without it cascading out of control (precisely what the Conservatives worry about).

If the CCP does not turn in this direction, though, the regime will sink deeper and deeper into stagnation and will decline over time.

Some observers, myself included, believe that the CCP's endgame has already begun (unless there is a return to Soft Authoritarian political reform). Under this situation, the Party's authority and instruments of control progressively atrophy; it is a *protracted process—not* an immediate implosion. Many readers misunderstood the argument in my *Wall Street Journal* article in this regard.[43] I was not predicting an imminent *collapse,* but rather the protracted decline of the regime. Some autocratic regimes are overthrown from above by coup d'état or factional infighting, some are overthrown from below as a result of civil war or social revolution, and occasionally the ruling authoritarian leader or elite orchestrate a democratic opening from above (as occurred in Taiwan).[44] But many authoritarian regimes simply corrode and atrophy from *within,* like someone who has progressive cancer. When this occurs, such as in China now, observers should keep their eyes on the regime's instruments of control and those who have to enforce control. Citizens and party members alike are already complying insincerely with Party dictates. But the regime's propaganda agents and its internal security apparatus may become lax in enforcing the Party's writ. They may even begin to sympathize with dissidents, like the Stasi agent in the Academy Award–winning German film *The Lives of Others* (*Das Leben der Anderen*) who came to sympathize with the targets of his spying. This is not abstract Hollywood imagination—such Leninist regimes very often corrode from within and collapse under their own weight and ossified inefficiencies. Repression—like chemotherapy for someone who has cancer—can work for a while, but not forever.

Semi-Democratic Breakthrough

There is a fourth possibility. This would entail a real opening of the political system to embrace many of the elements and attributes of the semi-democratic systems currently operating in Hong Kong and especially Singapore. Under this possibility a CCP-dominant system remains in power, but it is one in which power is devolved and shared with other lesser parties; civil society exists (within limits); a competitive multiparty system functions with regular elections; fully autonomous legislative and judicial institutions exist alongside a professional civil service, and a relatively open media operates. Basic civil and human rights are respected, and citizens enjoy considerable protected freedoms within a constitutional framework. It is not democracy as it is known in the West (indeed it operates more efficiently). Under this model, the CCP would remain the dominant ruling party in power—just like the People's Action Party in Singapore. In recent years, the PAP has been challenged, and suffered its worst electoral results in history in the 2011 elections (garnering only 60 percent of the popular vote), before rebounding in the 2015 election by winning 70 percent of the votes and 83 of 89 seats in Parliament. Even Singapore has rid itself of the more draconian aspects of its authoritarian past.

For China to go down this semi-democratic path would still require a significant and far-reaching transformation of its current political system, which it may well not be capable of. It would really require fundamental changes in the way that the CCP currently operates. It would require empowering all citizens with the right to vote. It would require elections between competing parties; China already has eight so-called "democratic parties" (民主党派) which could be allowed to compete with each other and the CCP. It would require making the judiciary and National People's Congress autonomous branches of government from the CCP. It would require a variety of measures of policymaking transparency. It would mean that CCP cells *not exist* within government organs or enterprises. It would require a civil service whose personnel were not appointed by the CCP. It would require public asset declarations by government officials at all levels. It would require that government officials and budgets were subject to review by the parliament (NPC). It would require a military that was statutorily responsible to the government and not the CCP. It would require a free and open media. At a minimum it would require these elements of a democratic system, even if the CCP was the dominant (hegemonic) party. Would the CCP be willing to undertake these changes and subject itself to such constraints on its current complete monopoly of power? The chances are unfortunately close to zero, in my estimation.

Given this range of possible political pathways for China, I would estimate that Hard Authoritarianism will prevail until the Nineteenth Party Congress in 2017. After that the chances of a return to Soft Authoritarianism will rise, given the turnover of personnel described above, although it likely will not prevail. If it does not, then secular stagnation will continue, the reforms will continue to stall, and the CCP will gradually lose its grip on power.

China's Future and the World

What will be the nature of China's interactions with the world in the future? Will it be a benign partner and good neighbor, or an insular self-preoccupied country, or a threatening big power (or a combination)? Will its behavior reflect confidence and security, or defensiveness and insecurity? How will China's domestic evolution and the four future pathways identified in chapters 1–4 become manifest in its foreign relations? Conversely, how will the country's external environment impact its internal situation and shape the leaders' choices of these alternative pathways? Or, to what extent, do China's foreign relations operate based on a set of factors that are largely disconnected from the domestic issues discussed in previous chapters? We explore all of these questions in this chapter.

As China becomes an increasingly international actor and power, its global relationships are becoming more complicated and strained. This is natural, and it can be expected to continue indefinitely into the future. While China's government rhetorically pursues "win-win" relationships and a "principled foreign policy" built on "Peaceful Development" and the "Five Principles of Peaceful Coexistence,"[1] it inevitably encounters unanticipated situations and nations that do not view China in such a benign light. One factor is that the Chinese government does not control many of the actions of its commercial actors or citizens abroad, some of which are engaging in exploitative or illegal behavior. This is increasingly apparent in the developing world. Chinese cyber hacking and espionage are also now regular occurrences in the developed world. China's growing military capabilities and expanding naval footprint are beginning to alter regional security balances. China's huge financial resources and its "go global" (走出去) policy are having an economic impact everywhere on the planet, not always positive. Its ambitious space program includes an orbiting space station, a large satellite program, and plans to land men on the moon between 2020 and 2025.

All of these developments are affecting international relations, as well as China itself. Not surprisingly, the most intensive region of interaction for China is its own neighborhood. Situated at the heart of Asia, China borders fourteen other nations on land and several more by sea. Given China's central geographic position and sheer size, its rising nationalism, its strong military, its huge economy, and its disputed territorial claims, it is not surprising that China is experiencing growing difficulties and tensions with its neighbors.

Rising Tensions on China's Periphery

The sources of such tensions and strategic distrust vary by country vis-à-vis China, but there are only a handful of countries in Asia that are *not* experiencing tensions with Beijing.[2] These rising tensions can be expected to remain and even intensify in the years ahead.

South Korea probably has the strongest and most positive relationship with China, but even Seoul is not content with Beijing's handling of North Korea and its provocative behavior. South Korea is also not pleased with China's depictions of its history and geography. Meanwhile, China-North Korea relations are also severely strained, as

Beijing has tried to demonstrate its displeasure with Pyongyang since Kim Jong-un came to power. South Korea is behaving like a good tribute state, but North Korea is not.

Japan-China tensions have multiple sources, run very deep, and show only minimal signs of amelioration. Public perceptions of China in Japan are at an all-time low (7 percent favorable). Japan now sees China as its leading national security threat, and the revision of Article IX of its Constitution is stimulated in large part by this growing sense of China as a threat. Although a diplomatic "floor" may be established under the deeply distrustful and strained Sino-Japanese relationship, and commercial interactions continue, rivalry between these two leading regional powers will be a permanent feature of the Asian strategic landscape for many years to come. As long as the rivalry exists and the relationship is dysfunctional, Asia as a whole is strategically unstable.

China's relations with Taiwan, despite remarkable and positive progress in cross-strait relations over the past eight years, are still deeply afflicted by Taiwan's separate identity and fear of being absorbed into the mainland's grasp (see chapter 3). The growth of ties has meant substantially increased economic dependence of the island on the mainland, something many Taiwanese are not comfortable with. Taiwan also lives daily under a huge military threat from the mainland, including over 1,200 short-range ballistic missiles aimed at the island twenty-four hours a day, 365 days a year.[3]

In Southeast Asia, the Philippines, Vietnam, Malaysia, and Brunei are all embroiled in territorial disputes with China in the South China Sea. This multilateral dispute has strained Beijing's bilateral relations with each country, as well as collectively with the Association of Southeast Asian Nations (ASEAN). Cambodia is as close to being a client state of Beijing's as exists in Asia, but even there the country is beginning to show signs of choking under Beijing's smothering

economic embrace and diplomatic pressure.[4] Myanmar experienced
the same suffocation until it drew back from Beijing's grasp in 2011;
since then a variety of bilateral frictions have continued to fray relations. China's damming of the Irrawaddy River was the main catalyst
for the Myanmar government to pull back, although the sprawling
Chinese presence throughout the country was the underlying factor.
China's damming of the upper Mekong River may have a similar effect
with Laos. Thailand and Indonesia are the only two ASEAN states that
have seemingly smooth relations with China today, but there have
been historical frictions in each case that could resurface.

New Zealand has also become economically dependent on the
China market (particularly in agriculture and dairy), and Wellington
is nervous about China's forays into the South Pacific islands, which
it considers its backyard. Chinese cyber hacking and large-scale land
purchases of rich agricultural land on the South Island are also beginning to raise hackles in New Zealand's media and parliament.[5] For its
part, Australia has a similarly economically dependent relationship
with China, while the national security community in Canberra is
deeply divided over whether China constitutes a military threat to the
region and its own security.

In South Asia, India maintains a modicum of normalcy in its ties with
China, but not far under the surface reside deep anxieties and fears of
China militarily and geopolitically. Historical memories dating to the
1962 border war and the fact that China still occupies enormous tracts
of disputed territory continue to hang over the relationship. China's
dam building on the Tibetan Plateau is also affecting the Brahmaputra,
Indus, and Ganges rivers and is a further irritant for New Delhi, while
India's harboring of the Dalai Lama's exiled government has been a
longstanding aggravation for Beijing. China's steadfast support for
India's erstwhile adversary Pakistan has been perhaps the greatest

irritant to New Delhi over the decades. Sri Lanka is also undergoing a pullback in its relations with Beijing, very similar to what Myanmar experienced, owing to China's growing economic presence in the country.[6] Nepal is experiencing similar pains of over-dependency and discomfort with China's creeping presence in the Himalayan kingdom. Bangladesh remains China's second largest arms importer (after Pakistan) and is dependent on China for aid. Meanwhile, relations with Pakistan, China's "all-weather friend," remain as robust as ever. In 2015 Beijing bestowed an unprecedented $46 billion aid package on Islamabad, but that causes further frictions with India.

Further to the north, China's relations with the Central Asian republics appear very strong and sound, with energy and infrastructure investment greasing the wheels. China's announced "One Belt, One Road" initiatives, and the creation of the Asian Infrastructure Investment Bank,[7] will contribute $115 billion over the next decade to the entire Asian region—no doubt a very positive development in terms of much-needed infrastructure, but one wonders when the recipient nations may begin to chafe under the weight of the anticipated huge Chinese presence. There is also a real question of whether the huge aid assistance pledges will materialize. China does not have the best track record on following through on its promises. Over the past decade it promised close to $30 billion to Indonesia but only delivered about 7 percent of it.[8] This has been the case in many other countries across the developing world as well. Central Asia is also Russia's strategic backyard, which may affect relations between Moscow and Beijing. More likely, the landlocked Central Asian states will become adept at manipulating their neighboring powers and garnering resources from each.

Diplomatically, Beijing is proactively engaged throughout the Asian region, regularly convening bilateral and multilateral summits with regional leaders. When they meet, China's economic largesse follows.

China's Exports and Imports Across Asia						
	2011			**2012**		
Country	Total Trade	Imports from China	Exports to China	Total Trade	Imports from China	Exports to China
Brunei	1.3	0.7	0.6	1.6	1.3	0.4
Cambodia	2.5	2.3	0.2	2.9	2.7	0.2
Indonesia	60.6	29.2	31.3	66.2	34.3	32
Laos	1.3	0.5	0.8	1.7	0.9	0.8
Malaysia	90	27.9	62.1	94.8	36.5	58.3
Myanmar	6.5	4.8	1.7	7	5.7	1.3
Philippines	32.2	14.3	18	36.4	16.7	19.6
Singapore	63.7	35.6	28.1	69.3	40.7	28.5
Thailand	64.7	25.7	39	69.8	31.2	38.6
Vietnam	40.2	29.1	11.1	50.4	34.2	16.2
Hong Kong	283.8	268	15.5	341.3	323.4	17.9
Japan	342.5	148.3	194.6	329.5	151.6	177.8
South Korea	245.6	83	162.7	256.4	87.7	168.7
Australia	116.6	33.9	82.7	122.3	37.7	84.6
New Zealand	8.8	3.7	5	9.7	3.9	5.8
India	73.9	50.5	23.4	66.5	47.7	18.8

unit = 1 bn USD

Figure 5.1 China's Trade in Asia
Source: East by Southeast.

Money is the most important tool in China's foreign policy toolbox, and it is being utilized to an unprecedented extent. China is now the largest trading partner for every Asian nation except the Philippines, and the lion's share of its outbound investment remains in Asia.

There is no doubt that China has become the center of economic activity and supply chains in Asia (Figure 5.1). This is not by accident; it is very much by Beijing's design. The Chinese government calls this "economic interconnectivity." While it does benefit the region as a whole, it is also producing an increasing asymmetry and imbalance, and China's neighbors are beginning to chafe at the growing dependency on Beijing. Others, however, see the process as very natural and irreversible. Singapore's late leader and elder statesman Lee Kuan Yew, for example, observed in 2012: "China is sucking the Southeast Asian countries into its economic system because of its vast market and growing purchasing power. Japan and South Korea will inevitably be sucked in as well. It just absorbs countries without having to use force. . . . China's emphasis is on expanding their influence through the economy. China's growing economic sway will be very difficult to fight."[9] Viewed more broadly, though, China's share of regional trade and investment is far from being dominant. Beijing's investment in many Southeast Asian countries ranks below that of Japan, the European Union, or the United States, while its trade does not exceed 30 percent (usually 15 to 20 percent) of any individual Asian nation's total trade. All Asian countries maintain diversified commercial profiles. Nonetheless, hardly a conversation in any Asian capital does not reveal a growing sense of angst over China's economic heft and attempts to leverage it for other purposes. Beijing also seems to mistakenly believe that economic relations trump issues of identity or other troubled aspects of its ties with neighbors, which is not the case.

Added to the economic concern is China's dramatic military modernization and rapidly expanding naval presence throughout the Indo-Pacific region. The "string of pearls" is becoming a reality, as China is establishing a series of port-access arrangements all along the Indian Ocean littoral to east Africa. China and its paramount leader Xi Jinping have made it very clear that it intends to become a "maritime power" (海洋强国). By 2030 it is quite possible that China's navy could include five aircraft carriers. It already possesses the largest number of surface warships in the world (370). In 2015 China published its first White Paper on its military strategy, which explicitly identified the "strategic requirement of offshore waters defense and open seas protection." The Chinese distinguish between "near seas" (近海) and "far seas" (远海), the former being contiguous to China's coastline and the latter being open-ocean "blue water" operations. The White Paper indicated that the People's Liberation Army Navy (PLAN) "will gradu-

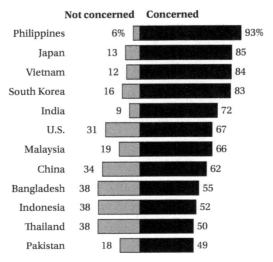

Figure 5.2 Asian Perceptions of China's Territorial Disputes
Source: Pew Research Center Global Attitudes Survey (Spring 2014).

ally shift its focus" from the former to the latter.[10] As the White Paper starkly said, "The traditional mentality that land outweighs sea must be abandoned." China's island-building in the South China Sea has also caused further wariness among China's southern neighbors, as its East China Sea claims have done in Japan. Beijing's unilateralism and dismissiveness of these concerns is further fueling regional anxieties. Polls of Asian nations conducted by the Pew Global Attitudes Project in 2014 and 2015 revealed widespread concerns across the region that China's territorial disputes could trigger conflict (Figure 5.2).

Thus, all around China's periphery, China's relationships are a combination of sweet and sour, but are increasingly souring. I would anticipate this becoming a secular trend that will continue over the next decade and beyond. What it is producing, and will continue to produce, is the Iron Law of International Relations: the law of counter-balancing. The Obama administration's "pivot to Asia" (or rebalancing policy) was no accident when it was unveiled—it was a direct result of the nervousness that America's allies and many other nations in Asia felt about an increasingly assertive China during 2009–2010. This balancing behavior will likely continue indefinitely. The stronger China becomes, the greater the fears, the greater the pushback and counter-measures. If Beijing is trying to recreate a twenty-first century version of the imperial tribute system, it will inevitably fail, as other sovereign Asian nations do not desire to fall into such a patron-client relationship with China again. China's geographic location in the center of Asia is actually a great weakness, as it enables such counter-balancing and encirclement responses.

China's Relations with Other Powers

China's relations with the world's other powers—America, Russia, and Europe—display three distinct patterns, all of which can be expected to continue over the coming decade. The relationship with the United States is increasingly fraught and competitive, the relationship with Russia is close and strategically expedient, while the relationship with the European Union is now maturing.

The Sino-American Conundrum: Competitive Coexistence

Relations between the United States and China have never been easy, but they are getting much more complicated and strained. The areas of bilateral and global cooperation have shrunk in recent years, while the realms of growing discord and competition have steadily increased. This is not an aberration or a temporary trend; it is the "new normal." It is also entirely natural and predictable. As China's comprehensive power grows, its sense of self-importance becomes more apparent.

Sometimes Beijing's rhetoric borders on hubris, driven by its own powerful nationalism. As China's interests and presence have expanded around the globe,[11] it is increasingly bumping up against the United States in faraway regions where it has never been present before—but the fulcrum of the two powers' interactions and strategic competition is in the Asia-Pacific region. To be sure, the national interests of China and the United States overlap in many regions, yet they seem unable to work together on a common agenda in Africa, Asia, the Middle East, or Latin America. Washington has tried to enlist Beijing as a global partner in a broad-gauged partnership in global governance (dubbed a "G-2" by some analysts), but this effort was rejected twice by China: in 2005 and 2009, although it seemed to make more progress at the 2014 and 2015 summit meetings between Presidents Barack Obama and Xi Jinping. For its part, Beijing—and President Xi Jinping personally—has sought to build a "new type of major country relation" (新型大国关系) with the U.S. government, only to have the Obama administration not pursue the concept. While a worthy goal, the U.S. administration argued that the relationship should be built on real actions and not slogans.

There are a number of reasons why the two powers find themselves locked into an increasingly competitive relationship. For one thing, it is entirely predictable that such intrinsic tensions should emerge between an established power and a rising, challenging power. History is filled with such cases—Harvard's Graham Allison describes this as the "Thucydides' Trap," in which eleven of the fifteen cases since 1500 have resulted in military conflict.[12] In today's political science parlance this is known as "power transition theory." One key finding of power transition theorists is that the chances of conflict become most acute when the rising power's aggregate power begins to come close to that of the predominant power—the crossover threshold point—a stage that some believe is now upon us. I am not one of those, as I see China's comprehensive power as still lagging significantly behind that of the United States. Economically, yes, China is drawing close to America's aggregate GDP (but certainly not per capita). Militarily, China has nuclear weapons and an increasingly oceangoing navy, as well as a threatening cyber capacity, but its military lags well behind American capabilities across the board. Moreover, China has only one ally (North Korea) while the United States has some sixty treaty allies around the globe.[13] *The Economist* estimates that of the 150 largest countries in the world, nearly 100 lean toward the United States, while 21 lean against it.[14] China has no military bases abroad; America's are extensive. China has minimal conventional military power projection capabilities; the United States military can deploy anywhere and anytime.

This is not to say that China's military has not made enormous advances,[15] or that it is not a potential threat to other nations in Asia and eventually beyond, or could still "pose problems without catching up" (in Thomas Christensen's well-chosen description of the PLA's asymmetric warfare capabilities), but overall there remains a huge gap between American and Chinese defense capabilities. China's cultural soft power lags even further behind. In a variety of areas in science and technology, higher education, and research and development the gap is also great.

For all of these reasons, in my last book, *China Goes Global*, I described China as a "partial power,"[16] and I remain mystified why there is an "illusion of Chinese power" held by many around the world.[17] Many readers will surely disagree with this assessment and dismiss my argument as typical American arrogance and ignorance, but I base my judgments on empirical facts, not subjective perceptions. China has a very, very long way to go before it catches up with the United States. Even other medium powers outstrip China: England, India, or South Korea have more soft power than China; Japan and

Germany have greater innovative capacity than China; while Russia's or NATO's military is more powerful in many respects.

Yet I am the first to agree that *perceptions matter,* and they matter greatly in international relations. I have spent my entire academic career, since writing my doctoral dissertation about Chinese perceptions of America,[18] emphasizing the role of perceptions. As the American sociologist W. I. Thomas poignantly observed nearly a century ago (1928): "If men define situations as real, they are real in their consequences."[19] Thus, it is important that many around the world *perceive* that China will overtake—or has already overtaken—the United States as the world's leading power. The 2014 Pew Global Attitudes Survey revealed that majorities in twenty-seven of forty nations surveyed believed that China will eventually replace, or already has replaced, the United States as the world's leading power (Figure 5.3).

These are important findings and should be taken seriously. China is clearly *seen* to be a world-class power—and there is an expectation that this power will only increase over time. Again, I am not so sure. If the negative domestic trajectories of China that we described

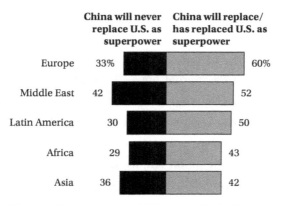

Figure 5.3 Perceptions of China as a Global Power
Source: Pew Research Center Global Attitudes Survey (Spring 2014).

in chapters 1–4 continue, the bloom may quickly wear off the rose of China's current positive global image. In fact, global surveys indicate it is already occurring. Involvement of China in a conflict would also undoubtedly tarnish its reputation. Overbearing Chinese diplomacy can also be damaging, while China's resource exploitation across the developing world is already producing a rising negative impression.

Perceptions of China in the United States (Figure 5.4) have been trending in an increasingly negative direction for some time. The 2013 Pew Global Attitudes Project surveyed publics in both countries and found that distrust is rising in both. In America, 68 percent of the general public and 80 percent of experts and scholars described China as a "competitor," while only 26 percent said China could "be trusted." The same survey found that 66 percent of Chinese respondents described

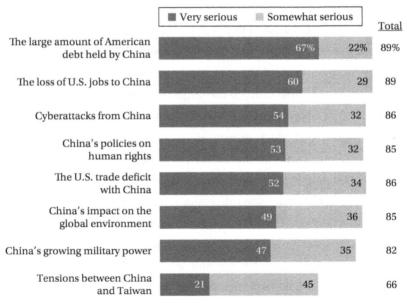

Figure 5.4 American Views of China, 2005–2015
Source: Pew Research Center Global Attitudes Survey (2015).

the U.S. as a "competitor" while 15 percent designated America as an "enemy." Thus, roughly two-thirds of both publics view U.S.-China relations as "competitive"—and this is a significant change since 2010, when a majority in both countries still had positive views of the other. In general, since 2012, more Americans see China unfavorably than favorably.

Despite increasingly negative perceptions, U.S.-China relations will be vitally important in the future. These two titans are tangled together in innumerable ways—strategically, diplomatically, economically, socially, culturally, environmentally, regionally, internationally, educationally, and in many other domains.[20] The two nations are the principal powers in the Asia-Pacific region and globally. The two possess the world's two largest economies on aggregate, two largest military budgets and navies, are the two largest consumers of energy and importers of oil in the world, are the two largest national emitters of greenhouse gasses and contributors to climate change, contribute the two largest numbers of PhD's and patent applications in the world, and are the only two true global actors on the world stage today. They are each other's second largest trading partner (nearly $600 billion in two-way trade), while China is the largest foreign creditor of the United States and its investment in the U.S. is growing rapidly (over $12 billion, employing 80,000 Americans in 2014). China is the world's largest exporting nation and the United States the largest importer. Every day about 9,000 people travel between the two countries, 300,000 Chinese students study in American universities, with about 20,000 Americans studying in China. There are 38 sister province/state and 169 sister city relationships binding localities together and offering opportunities for exchanges. There are 300 million Chinese learning English and approximately 200,000 Americans learning Chinese.

By these and many other measures, the United States and China are inextricably tied together. At the societal level, it is a thick and dense relationship—far deeper than many citizens in both countries may realize. At the governmental level there is no shortage of interaction. More than ninety separate bilateral dialogue mechanisms are in place, bringing officials together on a fairly regular basis. The problem is not so much with the *process* of the relationship as with its *substance*. The Sino-American relationship is finding it increasingly difficult to find a stable equilibrium—much less a positive narrative and trajectory into the future. An ever-expanding battery of problems buffet the relationship daily. The relationship has been fundamentally troubled for many years and has failed to find extensive common ground to forge a real and enduring partnership. The "glue" that seems to keep it together is the fear of it falling apart. There really has not been a strong bond holding the two nations together since the end of the Cold War during the mid-1980s. Without such a strategic anchor, the relationship is left vulnerable to unremitting frictions on second-tier issues. Maintaining peace, stability, and security in the Asia-Pacific region—the most dynamic region in the world—could provide shared strategic purpose, but the two nations' respective security postures are more competitive than complementary.

The macro trajectory for the last decade (at least) has been steadily downward—only punctuated by high-level summits between the two presidents, which temporarily arrest the downward trajectory and provide periodic hope of stabilization and improvement in the relationship. But these summits and bilateral meetings quickly prove to be short-lived and ephemeral, with only a matter of months passing before the two countries encounter new shocks and the deterioration resumes. This has been the recurring pattern since the two governments reengaged post-Tiananmen with the Bill Clinton–Jiang Zemin summits of 1997–1998.

The balance between cooperation and competition has

progressively shifted over the past twenty years, with competition now becoming the dominant factor. There are several reasons for it—but one is that security increasingly trumps economics in the relationship. What is going on in the military, security, and geopolitical realms are now the dominant issues in the relationship—and it is almost exclusively a bad news story. In the United States what this means is that the "pro-engagement coalition" led by the business community is no longer dominant, and a "competition coalition" comprised of several constituencies is now asserting itself. Indeed, even the tone of the business community is shifting as American multinational corporations are encountering ever-greater bureaucratic impediments in China, operating costs are rapidly rising, while profit margins are shrinking.[21] As a result, the discourse in the American policy community underwent a notable shift in 2015. An unprecedented outpouring of commentary and reports spewed out of Washington think tanks that year and they were almost all negative in the way they portrayed China and U.S. policy towards China—all calling for a reevaluation of American policy, and most seeking a tougher policy across the board.[22] The 2016 presidential election campaign only serves to accentuate this trend. No matter who takes the oath of office and becomes the 45th President of the United States in January 2017, there will likely be a qualitative hardening of American policy toward China and thus a further descent in the relationship. This is a long-term secular trend and other actors in the world should not be surprised.

While China does its part to contribute to the fraying of ties, it must be said that there are some uniquely American sources of this deterioration. The disillusion with China in America probably says much more about the United States than it does about China. It is the latest chapter in America's two-century-long quest to influence China's evolution. Previous attempts, particularly during the Nationalist era (1911–1949), ended tragically with the "Who Lost China?" debate, scapegoating, and witch-hunting. Over the past two centuries one repetitive pattern has been consistent: America's "missionary impulse" to transform China in its image has repeatedly been disappointed by not understanding the complexities on the ground in China and by China's stubborn unwillingness to conform to American expectations.[23] Thus, the latest round of disillusion may have more to do with the United States and its unrealistic expectations than with China. History may be repeating itself again.

It may strike many readers as naïve in the extreme, but China is not turning out as many Americans—including the foreign policy community, U.S. Government, and a variety of nongovernmental actors—had anticipated and have worked hard for several decades to achieve. In essence, the "engagement" strategy pursued since President Nixon across eight consecutive administrations was premised on three pillars:

1. As China economically modernized it would liberalize politically.

2. As China's role in the world grew it would become a "responsible stakeholder" (in Robert Zoellick's famous words) in upholding the global liberal order created by the West and United States after the Second World War. America's (and Europe's) strategy was to embed China in this global institutional order (this was known as the "integration strategy") and thereby socialize it into the underlying liberal norms of the Western-created postwar order.

3. That China would not challenge the American-dominant security architecture and order in East Asia, and it would thus be a "status-quo" power.

The first premise is clearly not occurring—quite to the contrary. As China grows stronger economically it is becoming *more*—not less—

repressive politically and socially. There are any number of examples identified in chapters 3 and 4. Repression in China today is the worst it has been in twenty-five years, since the aftermath of the Tiananmen Incident of 1989. With respect to the second and third premises, we are not witnessing (at least not yet) frontal assaults by China on these regional and global institutional architectures; indeed, it would not be wise for China to do so, and China is not the kind of country that goes about things in a "frontal manner" (that is how Americans do things). But we are witnessing Beijing establishing a range of alternative institutions that clearly signal China's discomfort with the Western postwar order. Examples include the New Development Bank (organized by China together with the BRICS states), Asian Infrastructure Investment Bank (AIIB), the Shanghai Cooperation Organization, the Forum on China-Africa Cooperation, the China-Arab Cooperation Forum, the China-Central and Eastern Europe Leaders Meeting, and others. Finally, China's sustained decades-long military modernization program, which has been fueled by 12 percent *average* annual budget increases,[24] is altering the security environment in the Asia-Pacific region where the United States has enjoyed unrivaled preeminence since 1945. China also regularly rhetorically denounces the U.S. alliance system in the region, and its assertive moves to enforce its disputed maritime claims are changing "facts on the ground" (indeed, they are literally creating ground from submerged atolls it controls in the South China Sea) and directly challenging key American allies.

Hence, all three of the core premises that have undergirded more than four decades of American China policy are unraveling and coming under increasing criticism in Washington. In Beijing too, the United States is explicitly viewed as a subversive threat to Communist Party rule and an existential threat to China's security. China's "hawks" are even more vituperative than America's.[25] In such an environment, in which perceptions are mirror-imaged and actions are seen to be challenging the other's core national interests, it should be no surprise that Sino-American relations have deteriorated to a serious degree. It is the "new normal"—both sides and the entire world need to get used to it. This Sino-American comprehensive competition will probably be the most significant geopolitical factor in international affairs for the next decade and beyond.

Consequently, the key responsibility—and the key test—for both countries is to learn how to *manage competition*—what I call "competitive coexistence"—to keep it from edging toward a fully adversarial relationship and conflict, while trying to expand the zone of genuine cooperation (recognizing that complete accord is illusory and impossible). Unfortunately, neither country has a playbook to guide such a complex relationship (the Cold War did not include such interdependence and the Soviet Union was not integrated into the international order). Henry Kissinger envisions what he calls "co-evolution" between the two powers,[26] but even he concludes that this will require "wisdom and patience." It will also require mutual pragmatism, acceptance, and tolerance. Yet, it is not at all clear to me that the respective political cultures and existing political systems, national identities, social values, and worldviews will afford such a strategic Grand Bargain today. Thus, in the future, these two great nations are likely to find it increasingly difficult to coexist—yet they must. However complicated and fraught, this is a marriage in which divorce is not an option. Divorce = War.

The Dragon and the Bear Redux

By contrast, Beijing and Moscow currently enjoy the best relationship they have had in six decades. This is a good thing. The world should not wish that these two powers and giant neighbors be locked in antagonism. When this occurred during the 1960s–1980s it was highly dangerous and destabilizing. Beginning in the mid-1980s the former Soviet leader Mikhail Gorbachev and Deng Xiaoping orchestrated a series of mutual confidence-building steps to improve relations (which culminated in the renormalization of relations in 1989). Despite a brief hiatus following the collapse of the Soviet Union, the two sides continued their efforts to reduce sources of friction and rebuild their ties. A series of bilateral agreements were agreed to during the mid- to late 1990s, with the capstone being the 2001 Treaty of Neighborliness and Friendly Cooperation. Then in 2005 and 2008 the final impediment to ties was removed with twin agreements to formally demarcate their long-disputed 4,300-kilometer common border.

This set the stage for significant growth in the relationship over the past decade. Trade grew from a negligible $10 billion in 2003 to almost $100 billion in 2014, before sliding back in 2015 (due largely to declining energy and commodity prices). The two sides have set a goal of $200 billion by 2020. While still not in the league of China's trade with the European Union, United States, Japan, South Korea, or the ASEAN nations, it is now reaching a respectable level. It will continue to grow steadily in the future as long as the Chinese economy and energy demand continue to grow. The two countries have essential economic complementarities—Russia has oil, gas and raw materials, while China offers technology and consumer goods. But if Chinese demand for imported energy and raw materials declines in conjunction with a contracting industrial economy, so too will bilateral trade. The contraction of the Russian economy is also a factor. Russia also sells China weapons and transfers defense technology, although this defense trade has fallen considerably from a high of $3 billion annually to under $1 billion today. A master plan has also been concluded to develop 205 "major cooperation projects" in China's northeast (东北)

Figure 5.5 Presidents Xi Jinping and Vladimir Putin
Source: Wikimedia.

which is contiguous to the Russian Far East (eastern Siberia), although this initiative has not progressed. Thus, the economic aspect of China-Russian relations is, in fact, mixed.

The diplomatic relationship is better (Figure 5.5). The two leaders—Vladimir Putin and Xi Jinping—hold summits twice annually, and each was the other's honored guest for the military parades held in Moscow and Beijing in 2015 to commemorate the end of World War II.

The two autocratic leaders see eye-to-eye on a variety of international issues. Their two nations find considerable common cause in their mutual opposition to the United States and NATO. They regularly coordinate their positions in the United Nations Security Council and are not afraid to veto resolutions agreed to by the other P-5 members (U.S., U.K., and France), particularly when it involves military intervention in third countries. The two militaries also frequently partner in joint exercises, including unprecedented naval exercises recently in the Mediterranean Sea and Sea of Japan. Putin's 2015 intervention in Syria and 2014 annexation of Crimea disturbed Beijing, as did its 2008 intervention into Georgia, but no public condemnations were made.

Despite these commonalities and strategic coordination, there still remains an undercurrent of historical suspicion as well as contemporary irritants. A subterranean debate simmers in policy circles in Moscow about China's long-term intentions in Central Asia and whether China is manipulating Russia for its own strategic and development purposes.[27] There are some observers of the relationship who see it as entirely tactical and expedient, and they predict that the residue of historical distrust will again emerge to pit the two Eurasian powers against each other.[28] Other observers believe that the current positive relationship is more than a tactical marriage, runs quite deep, and is likely to endure for some time into the future. Just as U.S.-China competition will be an indefinite feature in international relations over the coming decade(s), a China-Russia strategic partnership to counter the United States and the Western liberal order will similarly remain a core feature of global geopolitics. The "strategic triangle" may be returning.

The China-European Marriage

China-Europe relations have been on something of a rollercoaster for the last twenty years.[29] The relationship has evolved like that of a newlywed couple who were romantically entranced with each other and had unlimited aspirations for their partnership together, into a difficult phase when the intensity of interactions produced unanticipated frictions and disappointed expectations, into a period of brief estrangement, until the two made the decision to stay together and pragmatically build on what they shared in common.

From the end of the Cold War and the collapse of former communist party-states in Eastern Europe in 1989 through 2006, relations at the bilateral and multilateral European Union level developed rapidly and comprehensively. Extensive ties were built up in all spheres—commercial, diplomatic, educational, cultural, scientific, and others. Only lacking were linkages in the defense and security realm (largely owing to the EU arms embargo and prohibitions in dealing with the Chinese military after 1989), although their respective space programs did cooperate. Economic ties led the way, with trade growing sixty-fold. By 2010 the EU collectively had become China's leading trading partner by volume, while China ranked second for Europe after the United States. The EU also became a leading aid donor to China. By 2003 things were developing so well that the two sides proclaimed a "comprehensive strategic partnership."

This was the honeymoon phase of the relationship. But like all marriages, the more the two interacted, the more differences and frictions inevitably surfaced. After a decade of rosy rhetoric and expanding ties, relations turned sour between 2006 and 2010. In October 2006, the European Commission in Brussels published a highly critical policy paper taking China to task over a broad range of issues (I was in the room in Brussels when it was released and saw the shock on the faces of Chinese present as they read the document).[30] Beijing took umbrage. Bilateral frictions subsequently flared with the Czech Republic, Denmark, France, Germany, and the United Kingdom. European public opinion of China began to plunge, becoming the most negative anywhere in the world (still the case to this day). European media and think tanks chimed in by publishing critical articles and studies,[31] while national parliaments began to debate about their ties to China. EU officials became increasingly outspoken and critical of China. As the EU Ambassador to China, Serge Abou, observed in an interview with me in early 2010: "We are not in a comfortable situation with China. There is a deep feeling of mutual frustration between the EU and China. China is not at all helpful or responsive to our concerns. Our dialogues are more like monologues."[32]

This deterioration lasted until 2011, when both sides took proactive steps to try and stabilize and rebuild relations. Economic imperatives again led the way. Since the global financial crisis of 2008 Europe has found itself mired in economic stagnation, and therefore China has become increasingly important—some would say vital—to the EU's economic recovery and growth. The two sides trade more than €1 billion per day, reaching a cumulative total of €467.3 billion ($527.7 billion) in 2014.[33] Chinese investment into the EU has also surged €49 billion ($55.3 billion) since 2009.[34] This accelerated rate of investment is due to continue over the next decade. Chinese investors are scouring the continent for property, potential corporate buyouts, and investment opportunities. The United Kingdom leads the way, where China has pledged to invest £105 billion ($162 billion) into building infrastructure alone between 2015 and 2025.[35] Chinese students are also flooding into Europe, with over 200,000 across the EU (150,000 in the U.K. alone), where the cost of tuition is much less expensive and the length of degree programs shorter than in the United States. China has also unleashed a wave of cultural exchanges in an attempt to repair negative perceptions in European societies. All major European heads of state make regular pilgrimages to Beijing (German Chancellor Angela Merkel has done so nine times), with Chinese Premier Li Keqiang and President Xi Jinping making high-profile visits in return. The diplomatic engagement is intensifying. At the EU level there are over sixty intergovernmental dialogue mechanisms as well as an annual summit. The EU-China relationship does not lack in exchanges or process; if anything, there is growing "dialogue fatigue" among

European governments. There continues, however, to be a dearth of defense and security exchanges, as the EU arms embargo remains in place. Also, the Tibet issue and China's human rights record remain sensitive issues in Europe.

Looking to the future, we can expect commerce to continue to power the China-Europe relationship. There are many economic complementarities driving the two sides together, but the commercial relationship is not symmetrical. European multinationals face growing impediments to their investments and operations in China, and the European Chamber of Commerce in Beijing is increasingly gloomy about the current and future outlook.[36] Europe's trade deficit of €137.7 billion in 2014 ($155.5 billion) is also a nagging concern. Despite this point of friction, the relationship is not plagued by the Taiwan issue or strategic concerns in Asia, as is the case in Sino-American relations. Nor is the EU as preoccupied with China's role in global governance as previously. Having punished several European countries for their meetings with the Dalai Lama, Beijing also seems to have successfully drawn a line on the Tibet issue that European leaders are now loathe to cross. All of these reasons permit the two sides to focus on commercial and other exchanges. Now that the two sides have worked through the difficulties in the middle of their marriage, they seem to have found pragmatic and more mature ways of interacting.[37]

The Global South: Fraternity or Neo-Colonialism?

The developing world has always held a special place in Chinese foreign policy. Dating back to the 1954 Geneva Conference on Indochina and the 1955 Afro-Asian Conference in Bandung, Indonesia, the People's Republic of China has long prioritized its relations with developing countries. This prioritization was based on a sense of common history and identity growing out of these nations' struggles with imperialism and colonialism. Thus it can be said that the original impetus for China's ties to what Mao called the "Third World" was *ideational*, but this soon morphed into an *ideological* bond as well during the 1960s-1970s, as China began actively to support, arm, and train various "national liberation movements" across the developing world. In 1964 Premier Zhou Enlai, while touring Africa, proclaimed the continent "ripe for revolution." Beijing's attempts to export revolution to insurgencies in these far-flung regions, and to overthrow established governments, was clearly behavior of a non–status quo power. It particularly alienated China's neighbors in Southeast Asia, where it left a long residue of distrust that has not fully disappeared to this day.

Although China abandoned exporting revolution in the late 1970s, the developing world has remained a high priority in Beijing's diplomacy, cultural ties, commerce, and (increasingly) security. In multilateral organizations such as the United Nations, China maintains common cause by voting about 80 percent of the time together with developing countries in the General Assembly.[38] It has established a variety of international institutions, regional organizations, and dialogue groupings, such as the New Development Bank (a project organized by China together with Brazil, Russia, India, and South Africa), the Asian Infrastructure Investment Bank (AIIB), the Shanghai Cooperation Organization (SCO), Forum on China-Africa Cooperation (FOCAC), the China-Arab Cooperation Forum (CACF), and the China-Community of Latin American and Caribbean States Forum. While not an institution, one of China's biggest initiatives has been the so-called "One Belt, One Road" project to build infrastructure and facilitate commercial "connectivity" from northwest China across Eurasia and from southeast China to Africa and the eastern Mediterranean. Through these initiatives, China is meticulously constructing an alternative and parallel global institutional architecture to the postwar Western order. This is motivated by Beijing's longstanding dissatisfaction with what it perceives to be inherent pro-Western biases of the post–World War II institutional architecture, as well as its longstanding desire to give greater voice to developing countries. Beijing describes its goals as the "democratization of international relations" and creating a "multipolar" world order.

In terms of bilateral diplomacy, the Chinese government expends enormous time and resources cultivating and building ties with developing countries. A steady stream of heads of state passes through the Great Hall of the People in Beijing every year, while China's own leaders and top officials pay regular visits to Southeast, South, and Central Asia; Africa and the Middle East; and Latin America and the Caribbean. With all of these regions and countries, China's financial largesse has been on ample display in recent years. Beijing is showering Big Money—or at least the promises of it—across these regions: $50 billion for the AIIB, $40 billion for the Silk Road Economic Belt, $25 billion for the Maritime Silk Road, and $41 billion for the New Development Bank (out of $100 billion total initial capitalization). In addition, Beijing has pledged a $250 billion investment in Latin America and $1.25 trillion in the Asia-Pacific region, both by 2025. China's aid programs are also significant and generally do a lot of good. In terms of annual expenditure, China's aid is only about $3 billion per year—in the range of Australia, the Netherlands, or Denmark—but much more flows in the form of trade credits, training programs, and infrastructure construction, which do not appear on the official development assistance ledgers. Like China's military budget, a considerable amount of China's overseas assistance is concealed in other ministerial budgets (such as the

Ministry of Health, Ministry of Education, Ministry of Agriculture, Ministry of Foreign Affairs, Exim Bank, China Development Bank), while the Ministry of Commerce tellingly remains the lead agency. While China's "no strings attached" aid programs have come in for considerable and well-deserved criticism by Western countries and some international institutions for not conforming to international donor standards established by the OECD Development Assistance Committee, Chinese development assistance has nonetheless contributed a great deal to needy nations. China has filled voids and met needs not satisfied by the World Bank and other regional development banks. In Africa alone China claims to have completed 900 projects, 2,233 kilometers of railroads, 3,391 kilometers of highways, 42 stadiums, and 54 hospitals, dispatched more than 18,000 Chinese medical and public health personnel and 350,000 technicians, trained 30,000-plus Africans from various sectors, and offered 34,000 government-funded scholarships to African students.[39] China's work in public health, tertiary education, capacity training, and agriculture is particularly commendable.

The other major—and growing—component of China's ties to the developing world is trade. From 2000 to 2010 China's trade with nondeveloped Asia grew fortyfold, with Africa by 66 percent, with Latin America by 73 percent, and with the Middle East by 75 percent. While still a relatively small percentage of China's total global trade, these regions are becoming increasingly important export markets for China. Trade with both Africa and Latin America now both exceed $200 billion per year. China's merchandise exports to these regions are growing as China has found niche markets for various goods ranging from cars and trucks to consumer durables to applied technologies (notably telecommunications). This trend can be expected to continue, and to grow well into the future as Chinese exporters now enjoy new comparative advantages in the developing world. But the big driver in trade has been on the import side, as China has become deeply dependent on raw material commodities and energy imports to fuel its industrial boom. In 1993 China crossed the threshold to being a net importer of oil and is now the world's largest importer. By 2010 China was dependent on imports for more than half of its total consumption—4.8 million barrels per day (bb/d) of 9.2 million bb/d that year (costing the country $138.5 billion). China's oil consumption has been growing about 8 percent per year since 2002. The International Energy Agency projects that by 2030 China's oil demand will rise to 16.6 million barrels per day and its imports will reach 12.5 million bb/d.[40] However, a slowdown in China's industrial economy will surely affect these projections. The contraction of 2014–2015 has already markedly reduced imports of certain commodities, triggering a precipitous decline in global prices. If the government is able to transition to a new growth and development model as envisioned in the "rebalancing strategy" (see chapter 2), this too will contribute to reducing China's import demand.

China's presence in the developing world has not, however, come without its blemishes. The extraction of energy and raw materials has led to criticisms that China is behaving in a "neo-colonial" fashion. Africans in particular are saying, "We've seen this movie before." In the African case, though, the rising irritation is compounded by the huge number of Chinese businesses and people now resident across the continent. An estimated 1 million Chinese people and 8,000 commercial entities now live and operate in Africa.[41]

While China's overall "favorability" ratings in global public surveys remain quite strong and positive across the developing world, there has been a noticeable drop-off in recent years as the Chinese commercial presence has expanded. This was strikingly apparent in surprising

	Chinese music, movies and television			Chinese ideas and customs are spreading here		
	Like	**Dislike**	**DK**	**Good**	**Bad**	**DK**
	%	%	%	%	%	%
Argentina	11	68	21	28	55	17
Bolivia	37	44	19	30	51	19
Brazil	19	75	6	36	58	6
Chile	25	50	25	27	57	16
El Salvador	28	61	11	37	50	13
Mexico	19	56	25	27	55	18
Venezuela	38	58	4	37	51	12
Ghana	42	51	6	31	60	9
Kenya	36	45	19	54	34	11
Nigeria	54	32	14	58	24	18
Senegal	32	54	14	62	25	14
S. Africa	22	60	19	37	46	17
Uganda	28	46	26	31	46	23

Figure 5.6 China's Soft Power Appeal in the Developing World
Source: Pew Research Center Global Attitude Survey (July 2013).

results from a poll conducted by the Pew Global Attitudes Project on China's soft power in Africa and Latin America. As Figure 5.6 reveals, with the exception of Nigeria, China's soft power appeal was distinctly negative in twelve of the thirteen African and Latin nations surveyed (American soft power, by contrast, was overwhelmingly positive in the same poll).[42]

This survey supports other anecdotal evidence that China's earlier appeal may be wearing off. If so, this would conform with the same pattern we witnessed occurring with respect to Asia and Europe. Perhaps this is simply part and parcel of becoming a global power— not everyone is going to love you.

China's Growing Military Capabilities

Unlike China's soft power, which remains quite soft around the world,[43] its hard power is growing by the day. This was literally on display in massive military parades in Tiananmen Square on October 1, 2009 and September 3, 2015 (the former to commemorate the sixtieth anniversary of the PRC and the latter to commemorate the seventieth anniversary of the end of World War II).

China's military power is not a new phenomenon; it has steadily been built over the past quarter century. Fueled by a booming economy, China's military-industrial complex has been the beneficiary of annual budget increases in excess of GDP growth. From 1998 to 2007 China's GDP has averaged 12.5 percent growth, but its (official) defense spending grew at an average of 15.9 percent.[44] Since then it has leveled off at between 10–12 percent annual increases. Today, in 2015, this gives China the world's second largest military budget, at $145 billion. And this is the officially declared budget—other estimates place the real figure at anywhere from 5 to 50 percent higher. Assuming a 10 percent annual rate of increase, China's official military spending is projected to reach $217.5 billion by 2020 and $290 billion by 2025 (Figure 5.7).

All of this investment has bought impressive capabilities. The ground forces have been downsized, have become more mobile and multifunctional, and now operate better in joint operations with other units. The PLA Air Force has also improved significantly in qualitative terms, with the retirement of thousands of older aircraft, the addition of new generations of attack fighters and transports, the acquisition of in-flight refueling capabilities, better airborne command and control, and more rigorous training regimens. The PLA Navy has been the favored service, as noted above, and has benefitted from the addition of a vast

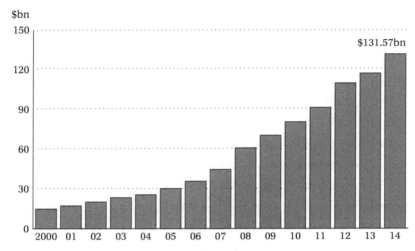

Figure 5.7 China's Military Spending 2000–2014
Source: State Council Information Office; Reuters.

number of new-generation surface combatants and submarines. The Navy's enhanced Marine Corps is an added asset. The strategic missile corps, or Second Artillery, has also benefitted from technical upgrading and modernization, including multiple warheads (MIRVs). The arsenal of short-range and medium-range ballistic missiles (SRBM and IRBM) have expanded in numbers and improved in accuracy. The intercontinental strategic forces, in the words of the White Paper on China's Military Strategy, "will strengthen its capabilities for strategic deterrence and nuclear counterattack, and medium- and long-range precision strike."[45]

All in all, China's military now have significant capabilities never before possessed. The steady pace and targeted scope of the modernization program has been strategically planned and executed. And there is no sign that the build-up will not continue over the next decade and beyond.[46] Military modernization will likely be immune from fluctuations in the economy or other domestic dislocations discussed in chapters 2–4. There is no evident "Guns vs. Butter" debate in China.

This progress noted, however, it should be said that the PLA has not had any real combat experience since 1979. Analysts also note various problems in China's military-industrial complex, the PLA's training regimen, its logistics system, and its C4ISR (command, control, communications, computers, intelligence, surveillance, and reconnaissance) capabilities. Then there is the serious problem of widespread corruption in the ranks; as of 2015, 4,024 officers (including 82 generals) had been netted in the anti-corruption campaign (including two former vice-chairs of the Central Military Commission).[47] In other words, while China's military hardware has improved markedly, its software still lags behind.

China's Future Impact on the World

China's trajectory will certainly have a global impact, no matter which future pathway it pursues. In the three previous chapters I have described a variety of alternative pathways that China's economy, society, and polity could take over the next decade and beyond. Essentially they all boil down to two most likely alternatives—Hard Authoritarianism vs. Soft Authoritarianism—and two lesser possibilities: Neo-Totalitarianism or Semi-Democracy. In terms of China's foreign relations, neither Hard nor Soft Authoritarianism would actually make much difference in China's regional and global posture. When it comes to foreign relations, I would anticipate much greater continuity in China's behavior irrespective of these two alternate future pathways. We must remember that foreign policy is an important means of preserving CCP rule and a source of legitimation for the regime. Under either Hard or Soft Authoritarianism, China's external ties will be used to bolster the regime. This will be increasingly the case as Chinese nationalism continues to be a key anchor of the regime's legitimacy.

However, should China take either of the two more extreme pathways—Neo-Totalitarianism or Semi-Democratic transition—it would have a greater impact. If China reverts to a neo-totalitarian path it would create even greater tensions with a variety of nations, notably Western and Asian countries. Such a turn toward much greater domestic political repression and state control of the economy could very conceivably be coupled with greater military aggressiveness in Asia and perhaps beyond. Tensions would rise significantly.

On the other hand, should China go down the (very unlikely) path toward Singapore-style democracy, it would alleviate underlying tensions with Asia and the West because of the intrinsic trust among democracies. I realize this is a controversial assertion for some, but I am a subscriber to "democratic peace" theory—the idea that democracies rarely fight democracies. Transparency and accountability—two hallmarks of democracy—intrinsically produce trust. Under such a scenario China would be welcomed as a member of the club of liberal democracies, and it would ratify, respect, and enforce the provisions in the United Nations Covenant on Civil and Political Rights (something Beijing has not done to this day). More broadly, China would be much more respectful of and adherent to the full body of norms embedded within global liberal institutions.[48] Beijing would likely no longer exhibit its ambivalent approach to global governance, which is premised on liberal norms and institutions.[49] Adopting such a semi-democratic political system in China, with all the attendant features described in chapter 4, would go far toward removing the core tensions in China's relations with other liberal nations (especially the United States).

At the same time, it would by no means resolve or alleviate the tensions with democratic Japan—as they are deeply rooted in Japan's Second World War aggression and postwar denial—or territorial disputes China has with its other neighbors (unless it abandoned its claims). Nor would a democratized China tamp down Chinese nationalism, pride, and identity as a great power. A semi-democratic China could be every bit as much—or more—of a military and diplomatic power in the world. But the underlying strategic distrust between China and many states would be alleviated, as they would share common liberal assumptions and approaches to world order. In addition to more humane and tolerant policies toward a wide range of civic actors in China, one would assume that a semi-democratic China would also adopt a much more lenient and inclusive approach toward Tibet and Xinjiang. Alas, the chances of this kind of China emerging over the next decade are regrettably minimal.

A key variable to consider is how the internal situation in China unfolds in the years ahead. This will have a large impact on the degree of confidence PRC leaders have in their ability to deal effectively with external relations. A more confident leadership less preoccupied with internal issues may be more prone to pursue China's ambitions—many of which are at odds with the United States and others. A less confident leadership preoccupied with internal problems could be less likely to take actions abroad. It is also worth noting that there is a large literature about "diversionary war" that suggests that embattled leaders at home (especially authoritarian ones) often provoke external conflicts to build domestic support. Given already hyper Chinese nationalism, this is not an impossibility.

In all likelihood, I anticipate that China's regional posture in Asia and (more broadly) internationally will look a lot like a continuation of the current situation—assuming a war does not break out between

China and the United States or between China and one or more of its neighbors. The possibility of war is not to be discounted. It is, in fact, a distinct possibility (the probability is not insignificant). Such a conflict could easily be triggered by an accidental military event, whereby escalation occurred rapidly absent high-level efforts and mechanisms to control it. This could occur vis-à-vis Japan, North Korea, Taiwan; vis-à-vis several of China's Southeast Asian neighbors, or India. In many of these cases the United States would quickly be drawn into the conflict (against China). It may even occur directly with the United States. The possibility of war involving China is the Black Swan event waiting to happen. I assess the possibility to be a lot higher than many would estimate, especially if triggered by a small-scale military encounter between China and one of its neighbors and/or the United States. One should not assume that it could not happen simply because it has not to date. Strategic tensions are already high and rising in East Asia, and they *all* relate to China.

Thus, looking to the future, China's role in the world can only be expected to increase regardless of which alternative domestic pathway it follows. The outstanding question is whether China gets along better or worse with the world. Two pathways we have identified—Neo-Totalitarianism and Hard Authoritarianism—can be expected to make China's foreign relations worse, while the other two pathways—Soft Authoritarianism or Semi-Democracy—could make them better. By selecting one of the latter two paths, China's leadership will have a greater chance of a "win-win" outcome—improving its chances of successful reforms at home and more cooperative relations abroad.

Notes

Preface

1. Many of these writings are captured in David Shambaugh (ed.), *The China Reader: Rising Power* (Oxford and New York: Oxford University Press, 2016). An interesting assessment of previous studies of China's future can be found in Roger Irvine, *Forecasting China's Future: Dominance or Collapse?* (London: Routledge, 2015). For China's perceptions of its future, see Daniel C. Lynch, *China's Futures: PRC Elites Debate Economics, Politics, and Foreign Policy* (Stanford, CA: Stanford University Press, 2015).
2. Roger Irvine, ibid.

Chapter 1

1. Xinhua, "Premier: China Confident in Maintaining Growth," March 16, 2007: http://news.xinhuanet.com/english/2007-03/16/content_5856569.htm.
2. Li Keqiang, "Report on the Work of the Government," delivered at the Third Session of the 12th National People's Congress, March 16, 2015: http://news.xinhuanet.com/english/china/2015-03/16/c_134071473.htm.
3. Xi Jinping, "Guanyu 'Zhonggong zhongyang guanyu quanmian tuijin yi fazhi guo ruogan zhongda wenti de jueding' de shuoming,"[Elaboration Concerning 'The Chinese Communist Party Center's Decision on Major Questions Concerning All-Around Development of a Nation Ruled by

Law'"], Xinhuanet, October 28, 2014, available at: http://cpc.people.com.
cn/n/2014/1028/c64094-25926150.html.

4. Minxin Pei, *China's Trapped Transition: The Limits of
   Developmental Autocracy* (Cambridge, MA: Harvard University Press,
   2006).

5. Available at: http://www.china.org.cn/china/third_plenary_
   session/2014-01/16/content_31212602.htm.

6. For one assessment of the Third Plenum's *Decision*, see my "Breaking
   Down China's Reform Plan," *The National Interest*, December 2, 2013:
   http://nationalinterest.org/commentary/breaking-down-chinas-
   reform-plan-9476. The discussion in this paragraph draws on this
   article.

7. USCBC China Economic Scorecard: https://www.uschina.org/reports/
   china-economic-reform-scorecard-february-2015.

8. European Chamber of Commerce in China, *Beijing Position
   Paper 2015/2016*: http://www.europeanchamber.com.cn/en/
   publications-local-position-paper.

9. Minxin Pei, *China's Trapped Transition: The Limits of Developmental
   Autocracy*, op. cit.

10. Ian Bremmer, *The J-Curve: A New Way to Understand Why Nations Rise
    and Fall* (New York: Simon & Schuster, 2006). See, in particular, chapter 6
    on China.

11. Daron Acemoglu and James A. Robinson, *Why Nations Fail* (New York:
    Crown Business, 2012).

12. Seymour Martin Lipset, *Political Man* (Baltimore, MD: Johns Hopkins
    University Press, 1963); Walt W. Rostow, *Politics and the Stages of Growth*
    (Cambridge: Cambridge University Press, 1962); A. F. K. Organski,
    The Stages of Political Development (New York: Alfred Knopf, 1965);
    and David Apter, *The Politics of Modernization* (Chicago: University of
    Chicago Press, 1965).

13. Samuel P. Huntington, *Political Order in Changing Societies* (New Haven:
    Yale University Press, 1968).

14. Ibid., p. 424.

15. Zbigniew Brzezinski, *The Grand Failure: The Birth and Death of
    Communism in the Twentieth Century* (New York: Charles Scribner
    & Sons, 1989), especially chapter 24. In fact, in Brzezinski's analysis,

degeneration and collapse had long been a distinct possibility for the Soviet bloc and it figured in his writings dating to the late 1960s. Brzezinski raised this possibility as early as 1956 in his classic work (with Carl Friedrich), *Totalitarian Dictatorship and Autocracy* (Cambridge, MA: Harvard University Press, 1956). A decade later he raised the possibility again in his "The Soviet Political System: Transformation or Disintegration?" *Problems of Communism* (January-February 1966), pp. 1–15.

16. See Charles Kupchan, *No One's World: The West, the Rising Rest, and the Coming Global Turn* (New York: Oxford University Press, 2013); Ian Bremmer, *Every Nation for Itself: What Happens When No One Leads the World?* (New York: Penguin, 2012).

17. National Intelligence Council, *Global Trends 2030: Alternative Worlds* (Washington, DC: National Intelligence Council, 2012).

Chapter 2

1. See David Shambaugh, *China Goes Global: The Partial Power* (New York: Oxford University Press, 2013), chapter 5.

2. See "China's Twelfth Five-Year Plan" (English Version): http://www.britishchamber.cn/content/chinas-twelfth-five-year-plan-2011-2015-full-english-version.

3. The World Bank and The Development Research Center of the State Council, People's Republic of China, *China 2030: Building a Modern, Harmonious, and Creative Society* (Washington, DC: The World Bank, 2013).

4. See, for example, Daniel H. Rosen, *Avoiding the Blind Alley: China's Economic Overhaul and Its Global Implications* (New York: The Asia Society Policy Institute, 2014).

5. Keira Lu Huang, "Xi Jinping's Reforms Encounter 'Unimaginably Fierce Resistance', Chinese State Media Says in 'Furious' Commentary," *South China Morning Post*, August 21, 2015; http://comments.caijing.com.cn/20150820/3951173.shtml.

6. See US-China Business Council, "USCBC China Economic Reform Scorecard—Marginal Improvement; Impact Still Limited," June

2015; ibid. (September 2015): https://www.uschina.org/reports/
uscbc-china-economic-reform-scorecard-september-2015.

7. See the discussion in Barry Naughton, "Economic Rebalancing,"
   in Jacques deLisle and Avery Goldstein (eds.), *China's Challenges*
   (Philadelphia: University of Pennsylvania Press, 2015).

8. I am grateful to David Lubin for his sense of the timing of the rebalancing
   program.

9. I am grateful to Pieter Bottelier for these insights.

10. http://data.worldbank.org/indicator/NY.GDP.PCAP.CD.

11. See Naughton, "Economic Rebalancing, op. cit., p. 117.

12. See Wing Thye Woo, "The Major Types of Middle Income Trap that
    Threaten China," in Wing Thye Woo, Ming Lu, Jeffrey D. Sachs, and
    Zhao Chen (eds.), *A New Economic Growth Engine for China: Escaping
    the Middle Income Trap by Not Doing More of the Same* (London and
    Singapore: Imperial College Press and World Scientific Publishing,
    2012).

13. Chen Changsheng and He Jianwu, "A Ten-Year Outlook," in Li Shijin and
    Development Research Center of the State Council Medium to Long-
    Term Growth Project Team, *China's Next Decade: Rebuilding Economic
    Momentum and Balance* (Hong Kong: CLSA Books, 2014).

14. Cited in Pieter Bottelier, "Is China's Economy Rebalancing?" speech
    at the Carter Center conference, "China's Reform—Opportunities and
    Challenges," May 6–7, 2015.

15. Interview, December 12, 2014, Beijing.

16. David Dollar, *China's Rebalancing: Lessons from East Asian Economic
    History* (Washington, DC: John L. Thornton China Center Working Paper
    Series, October 2013), p. 11.

17. Goldman Sachs Investment Strategy Group, *Emerging Markets: As the
    Tide Goes Out*, December 2013, p. 26.

18. See, for example, Nicholas Lardy, "False Alarm on a Crisis in China," *New
    York Times*, August 26, 2015.

19. *The Economist*, "Taking a Tumble," August 29, 2015, p. 20.

20. James T. Areddy and Lingling Wei, "China's Big Down-Shift," *Wall Street
    Journal*, August 26, 2015, A9.

21. See Wade Shepard, *Ghost Cities of China* (London: Zed Books, 2015).

22. I am grateful to David Lubin for this perspective.

23. See Kellee S. Tsai, "The Political Economy of State Capitalism and Shadow Banking in China," *Issues & Studies* (March 2015), pp. 55–97.

24. This system is well described in Carl E. Walter and Fraser J. T. Howie, *Red Capitalism: The Fragile Financial Foundation of China's Extraordinary Rise* (Singapore: John Wiley & Sons, 2011).

25. Pieter Bottelier, "Shadow Banking in China," unpublished paper, June 17, 2015. It should be noted, as Bottelier illustrates, that shadow banking is a *global*, and not just a Chinese, phenomenon. Total global shadow banking assets reached $73 trillion in 2013.

26. No author, "China's Path to Financial Deepening," *IFF China Report 2015* (London: Central Banking Publishers, 2015), p. 28.

27. The World Bank, *Reform Priorities in China's Financial Sector* (Washington, DC: The World Bank Group, 2015).

28. I thank Pieter Bottelier for pointing out these linkages.

29. Henry M. Paulson, Jr., *Dealing with China* (New York: Twelve Publishers, 2015), p. 338.

30. Richard Dobbs et al., "Debt and (Not Much) Deleveraging," McKinsey Global Institute Report, February 2015; Ana Swanson, "China's Increase in Debt Is Massive and Unsustainable," *Washington Post*, February 11, 2015; Zhiwu Chen, "China's Dangerous Debt," *Foreign Affairs* (May/June 2015), p. 11.

31. Dobbs et al., ibid.

32. "China Doubles Amount Set for Debt Swap," *Asian Wall Street Journal*, June 11, 2015.

33. Some analysts, such as Andy Rothman of Matthews Asia, dismiss the potential for local government defaults on debts (on the basis that the party-state will always step in to prevent this from occurring). See Andy Rothman, "Diagnosing China's Debt Disease" (San Francisco: Matthews Asia, May 14, 2015). Another leading research company (and Rothman's former employer), CLSA, has a more bearish take in their report *China Banks: Not Too Big to Fail* (Hong Kong: CLSA Ltd., 2015).

34. Tyler Durden, "The $8 Trillion Black Swan: Is China's Shadow Banking System About to Collapse?": http://www.zerohedge.com/news/2015-08-18/8-trillion-black-swan-chinas-shadow-banking-system-about-collapse.

35. Paul Krugman, "China's Naked Emperors," *New York Times*, July 31, 2015.

36. Enda Curran and Jeff Kearns, "With $21 Trillion, China's Savers Are Set to Change the World," *Bloomberg Business*, June 25, 2015.

37. See Peter Nolan, *Is China Buying the World?* (Cambridge: Polity Press, 2012); and David Shambaugh, *China Goes Global* (Oxford and New York: Oxford University Press, 2013).

38. Lingling Wei, "Controlled Ascent," *Wall Street Journal*, May 28, 2015.

39. "IMF Statement by Zhou Xiaochuan": http://www.imf.org/External/spring/2015/imfc/statement/eng/chn.pdf.

40. See James McGregor, *No Ancient Wisdom, No Followers: The Challenges of Chinese Authoritarian Capitalism* (Westport, CT: Prospecta Press, 2012).

41. No author, "China's Auditor Says State Firms Falsified Revenue and Profit," *Bloomberg Business*, June 28, 2015.

42. Patricia Cheng and Marco Yau, *China Banks* (Hong Kong, CLSA Ltd., 2015), p. 1.

43. Lingling Wei, "China Approves Push to Merge State Firms," *The Wall Street Journal*, September 8, 2015.

44. Nicholas Lardy, *Markets Over Mao: The Rise of Private Business in China* (Washington, DC: Peterson Institute for International Economics, 2014). Also see "Book Review Roundtable" in *Asia Policy* (July 2015), pp. 144–68.

45. Cited in David Zweig, "China's Political Economy," in William A. Joseph (ed.), *Politics in China* (New York: Oxford University Press, second edition, 2014), p. 268.

46. David Barboza, "Q&A: Nicholas Lardy on Markets and the State in China," *New York Times* (Sinosphere blog), May 15, 2015.

47. http://www.bloomberg.com/visual-data/best-and-worst//most-innovative-countries.

48. http://www3.weforum.org/docs/img/WEF_GCR2014-15_Innovation_Image.png.

49. Xi Jinping, "Transition to Innovation-Driven Growth," in Xi Jinping, *The Governance of China*, op. cit., p. 134.

50. Deng Yaqing, "Leaping Into the First Echelon," *Beijing Review*, April 23, 2015; "Route to a New Frontier," *Beijing Review*, June 4, 2015.

51. "Leaping Into the First Echelon," ibid., p. 13.

52. See Regina M. Abrami, William C. Kirby, and F. Warren McFarlan, *Can China Lead? Reaching the Limits of Growth and Power* (Cambridge, MA: Harvard Business School Press, 2014).

53. See, in particular, Daniel Breznitz and Michael Murphree, *Run of the Red Queen: Government, Innovation, Globalization, and Economic Growth in China* (New Haven: Yale University Press, 2011); and Michael T. Rock and Michael A. Toman, *China's Technological Catch-Up Strategy* (New York: Oxford University Press, 2015).

54. See Tai Ming Chueng (ed.), *Forging China's Military Might: A New Framework for Assessing Innovation* (Baltimore, MD: Johns Hopkins University Press, 2014); Tai Ming Cheung, *China's Emergence as a Defense Technological Superpower* (London: Routledge, 2012).

55. Personal conversations with several returnees.

56. Vanna Emia, "Chinese Government Considers Overseas Industrial Parks a Key Focus in Foreign Policy," *Yibad*, July 1, 2015; Jason Lange, "Chinese Firms Pour Money Into U.S. R&D in Shift to Innovation," Reuters, June 22, 2015; "R&D Road Leads to Universities in UK," *China Daily*, June 16, 2015.

57. See, for example, Can Huang and Naubahar Sharif, "Global Technology Leadership: The Case of China," *Science and Public Policy* (May 2015).

58. Minxin Pei, *China's Trapped Transition: The Limits of Developmental Autocracy* (Cambridge, MA: Harvard University Press, 2006).

59. See Daniel H. Rosen, *Avoiding the Blind Alley: China's Economic Overhaul and Its Global Implications* op cit, pp. 142–43.

60. See David Shambaugh, "The Coming Chinese Crack-Up," *Wall Street Journal*, March 7, 2015.

Chapter 3

1. *Forbes*, "The World's Millionaires and Billionaires," annual survey (2014).

2. Data from The World Bank *Social Development Indicators* (2014); CIA *World Factbook* (2014); State Council Information Office, *Progress in China's Human Rights in 2014*; State Council Information Office, *Gender Equality and Women's Development in China* (2005).

3. https://data.undp.org/dataset/HDI-Indicators-By-Country-2014/5tuc-d2a9.

4. See Richard Kraus, *Class Conflict in Chinese Socialism* (New York: Columbia University East Asian Institute, 1981).

5. A list of these is provided in David S. G. Goodman, *Class in Contemporary China* (Cambridge: Polity Press, 2014), pp. 14–15.

6. Ibid, p. 60.

7. See Shi Li and Terry Sicular, "The Distribution of Household Income in China: Inequality, Poverty, and Policies," *The China Quarterly* 217 (March 2014), figure 4, page 14.

8. David S. G. Goodman, *Class in Contemporary China*, op. cit., Table 2.1 (p. 59).

9. Cited in Sheng Sixin, "China's New Rich Posing a Challenge to Social Stability," in Wang Gungwu and Zheng Yongnian (eds.), *China: Development and Governance* (Singapore: World Scientific Publishing, 2013).

10. David S. G. Goodman, *Class in Contemporary China*, op. cit. Also see Yang Jing, "China's Middle Class: Still in the Making," in Wang Gungwu and Zheng Yongnian (eds.), ibid.

11. Dominic Barton et al., "Mapping China's Middle Class," *McKinsey Quarterly* (June 2013): http://www.mckinsey.com/insights/consumer_and_retail/mapping_chinas_middle_class.

12. Asian Development Bank, *Key Indicators for Asia and the Pacific 2010: The Rise of Asia's Middle Class* (Manila: Asian Development Bank, 2010), p. 8.

13. See: http://data.worldbank.org/indicator/SI.POV.GINI; http://english.people.com.cn/90778/8101702.html; https://www.quandl.com/collections/demography/gini-index-by-country.

14. See Jane Duckett and Guohui Wang, "Poverty and Inequality," in Jacques deLisle and Avery Goldstein (eds.), *China's Challenges* (Philadelphia: University of Pennsylvania Press, 2015), pp. 25–41.

15. Martin King Whyte, *The Myth of the Social Volcano* (Stanford: Stanford University Press, 2010), p. 197.

16. Dan Weihua, "Shehui zhuanxing qi shejing quntixing shijian de shencengci yuanyin fenxi [A Multilevel, Multicausal Analysis of Mass Incidents Related to Police During the Period of Social Transformation],"

Public Security Studies (*Gongan Yanjiu*), 2010, 10, pp. 23–28, esp. p. 25, as cited in Murray Scot Tanner, "China's Social Unrest Problem," Testimony Before the U.S.-China Economic and Security Review Commission, May 15, 2014: http://www.uscc.gov/sites/default/files/Tanner_Written%20 Testimony.pdf.

17. Jeremy Goldkorn, "*Legal Daily* Report on Mass Incidents in China in 2012," *Financial Times*, January 6, 2013.

18. See Harold M. Tanner, "The People's Liberation Army and China's Internal Security Challenges," in Roy Kamphausen, David Lai, and Andrew Scobell (eds.), *The PLA at Home and Abroad* (Carlisle, PA: U.S. Army War College Strategic Studies Institute, 2010), especially pp. 251–66. Quotation is from People's Armed Police Law, cited on p. 262.

19. See Gray Tuttle, "China's Race Problem: How Beijing Represses Minorities," *Foreign Affairs* (May/June 2015).

20. See Malte Philipp Kaeding, "Resisting Chinese Influence: Social Movements in Hong Kong and Taiwan," *Current History* (September 2015), pp. 210–16.

21. See: http://www.scmp.com/news/hong-kong/article/1636818/poll-finds-fewer-hongkongers-identifying-chinese-thanks-occupy?page=all.

22. See: http://www.savetibet.org/resources/fact-sheets/self-immolations-by-tibetans/

23. As cited in Yiyi Lu, *The Growth of Civil Society in China: Key Challenges for NGOs* (London: Chatham House Asia Program Briefing Paper, February 2005). Full Ministry of Civil Affairs national statistics are provided in Tables 1 and 2.

24. N.A., "Chinese Civil Society: Beneath the Glacier," *The Economist*, April 12, 2014.

25. Private conversations with two Chinese officials who witnessed this encounter, Beijing, autumn 2009.

26. "What Will This Crackdown Do to China's Nascent Civil Society?" *The Guardian*, January 24, 2015.

27. Edward Wong, "In War on Internet 'Troublemakers,' China Turns to Law on Picking Quarrels," *New York Times*, July 27, 2015.

28. See Edward Wong, "Chinese Leaders Approve Sweeping National Security Law, Bolstering Communist Rule," *New York Times*, July 1, 2015; Chun Han Wong, "China Imposes Sweeping National Security Law," *Wall*

Street Journal, July 2, 2015; N.A., "National Security: Everything Xi Wants," *The Economist*, July 4, 2015.

29. See Jon R. Taylor, "The China Dream Is an Urban Dream: Assessing the CPC's National New-Type Urbanization Plan," *Journal of Chinese Political Science* 20 (2015), pp. 107–20. The Plan was jointly issued by the CCP Central Committee and State Council.

30. The Chinese government has had the benefit of working closely with The World Bank, Asian Development Bank, and other international organizations in preparing its urbanization plan. See, for example, The World Bank and Development Research Center of the State Council, *Urban China: Toward Efficient, Inclusive, and Sustainable Urbanization* (Washington, DC: The World Bank Group, 2014).

31. Jonathan Fenby, *Tiger Head, Snake Tails: China Today, How It Got There and Where It Is Heading* (New York: The Overlook Press, 2012), p. 50.

32. Li Keqiang, "Report on the Work of the Government," Delivered at the Third Session of the Twelfth National People's Congress, March 16, 2015: http://news.xinhuanet.com/english/china/2015-03/16/c_134071473.htm.

33. http://www.chinahighlights.com/travelguide/top-large-cities.htm.

34. Luis Enriquez, Sven Smit, and Jonathan Ablett, *Shifting Tides: Global Economic Scenarios for 2015–2025* (September 2015), p. 5: http://www.mckinsey.com/insights/strategy/shifting_tides_global_economic_scenarios_for_2015_25.

35. http://www.telegraph.co.uk/news/worldnews/asia/china/8278315/China-to-create-largest-mega-city-in-the-world-with-42-million-people.html.

36. Ian Johnson, "As Beijing Becomes a Supercity, the Rapid Growth Brings Pains," *New York Times*, July 19, 2015.

37. See, for example, Premier Wen Jiabao's 2012 Government Work Report.

38. Zhang Fangzhu, "Eco-cities in China: A New Agenda of Planning for Sustainable Urban Development" (2014): http://www.regionalstudies.org/uploads/RSA_eco-city_china_Zhang_2014.pdf.

39. Li Shiqiao, *Understanding the Chinese City* (London: Sage Publications, 2014).

40. N.A., "Xi Jinping Isn't a Fan of 'Weird' Architecture in China," *Wall Street Journal*, October 17, 2014; Megan Willett, "Chinese President Xi Jinping: No More Weird Architecture," *Business Insider*, October 21, 2014.

41. Jeremy L. Wallace, *Cities and Stability: Urbanization, Redistribution, and Regime Survival in China* (New York: Oxford University Press, 2014).

42. Zhou Xian, "Urbanization: Quality More Important Than Speed," in Development Research Center of the State Council (ed.), *China's Next Decade: Rebuilding Economic Momentum and Balance* (Hong Kong: CLSA Books, 2014), p. 425.

43. For an excellent overview of the evolution of the *hukou* system see C. Cindy Fan, "Migration, *Hukou*, and the City," in Shahid Yusuf and Tony Saich (eds.), *China Urbanizes: Consequences, Strategies, and Policies* (Washington, DC: The World Bank, 2008).

44. Cited in Gabriel Wildau, "China Migration: At the Turning Point," *Financial Times*, May 4, 2015.

45. See Wang Hairong, "Ending Urban-Rural Dichotomy: China Unveils New Guidelines on Household Registration System," *Beijing Review*, August 14, 2014.

46. Wang Feng, "China's Population Destiny: The Looming Crisis," *Current History* (September 2010).

47. Wang Feng, "The Future of Demographic Overachiever: Long-Term Implications of the Demographic Transition in China," *Population and Development Review* 37 (2011 Supplement), p. 182.

48. As cited in Baozhen Luo, "China Will Get Rich Before It Grows Old," *Foreign Affairs* (May/June 2015), p. 20.

49. Ibid.

50. Luis Enriquez, Sven Smit, and Jonathan Ablett, *Shifting Tides: Global Economic Scenarios for 2015–2025* (September 2015), p. 5: http://www.mckinsey.com/insights/strategy/shifting_tides_global_economic_scenarios_for_2015_25.

51. Data from World Bank's World Development Indicators and China Data Online, as cited in Bruce Dickson, *The Dictator's Dilemma: The Chinese Communist Party's Strategy for Survival* (New York: Oxford University Press, 2016). I am grateful to my colleague Professor Dickson for sharing these data with me.

52. For an excellent overview of the health system reform plan see Qian Jiwei, "Reinventing China's Health System," in Wang Gungwu and Zheng Yongnian (eds.), *China: Development and Governance* (Singapore: World Scientific Publishing, 2013).

53. International Monetary Fund estimate, cited in Baozhen Luo, "China Will Get Rich Before It Grows Old," op. cit., p. 22.

54. Information Office of the State Council, *White Paper on Progress in China's Human Rights in 2014*, in *China Daily*, June 9, 2015; and Qian Jiwei, "Reinventing China's Health System," op. cit.

55. Cited in Shirley S. Wang, "Hospital Attempts Cultural Shift in China," *Wall Street Journal*, September 12–13, 2015.

56. Many of the specifics of this new pension program are described in Marc C. Dorfman et al., *China's Pension System: A Vision* (Washington, DC: The World Bank, 2013).

57. Mark W. Fraser, "What Happens When China Goes Gray," *The Diplomat*, January 14, 2014.

58. Baozhen Luo, "China Will Get Rich Before It Grows Old," op. cit., p. 22.

59. Information Office of the State Council, *Progress in China's Human Rights in 2014*, op. cit.

60. Baozhen Luo, "China Will Get Rich Before It Grows Old," op. cit.; Fraser, "What Happens When China Goes Gray," op. cit.

61. As cited in Zhu Jinping, "China Attracting Global Top Talent," in Wang Gungwu and Zheng Yongnian, *China: Development and Governance*, op. cit., p. 362.

62. Zheng Xin, "Chinese Students Abroad Face Academic Pressure," *China Daily*, June 2, 2015.

63. The Core-9 universities are: Peking University, Tsinghua University, University of Science and Technology of China, Nanjing University, Fudan University, Shanghai Jiaotong University, Zhejiang University, Xian Jiaotong University, Harbin Institute of Technology.

64. Zhao Litao, "China's Higher Education Reform," in Wang Gungwu and Zheng Yongnian (eds.), *China: Development and Governance*, op. cit., p. 373.

65. Source: *China Statistical Yearbook* (2013).

66. Yang Rui, "China Beware: A Corrupt Culture is Undermining Higher Education," *Global Asia* (Summer 2015), pp. 20–24.

67. Michael Sheridan, "Objection, Mr. Xi: Did You Earn That Law Degree?" *The Times of London*, August 11, 2013: http://www.thesundaytimes. co.uk/sto/news/world_news/Asia/article1298782.ece; Stephen

Thompson, "Plagiarism and Xi Jinping," *Asia Sentinel*, September 24, 2013: http://www.asiasentinel.com/politics/plagiarism-and-xi-jinping/.

68. Zheng Xin, "Chinese Students Abroad Face Academic Pressure," op. cit.

69. Some of this section draws on my book *China Goes Global: The Partial Power* (New York and Oxford: Oxford University Press, 2013). Also see Judith Shapiro, *China's Environmental Challenges* (Cambridge: Polity Press, 2012).

70. See Katherine Morton, *China and the Global Environment: Learning from the Past and Anticipating the Future* (Sydney: Lowy Institute for International Policy, 2009). Statistics are drawn from this and other studies.

71. Ed Crooks and Valentina Romei, "The G2: The Key to CO_2," *Financial Times*, December 9, 2009.

72. N.A., "The World's Most Polluted Places," *Time*, September 12, 2007.

73. N.A., "Raising a Stink," *The Economist*, August 5, 2010.

74. The World Bank, *Addressing China's Water Scarcity: Recommendations for Selected Water Resource Management Issues* (Washington, DC: The World Bank, 2009).

75. Asia Water Project, *In Deep Water: Ecological Destruction of China's Water Resources* (2007), as cited in Reuters, "China Says Water Supplies Exhausted by 2030," December 14, 2007.

76. Xinhua, "Half of China's Ground Water Contaminated," October 9, 2006, available at: http://www.china.org.cn/english/environment/183230.htm.

77. As cited in Andrew Jacobs, Javier C. Hernandez, and Chris Buckley, "Behind Deadly Tianjin Blast, Shortcuts and Lax Rules," *New York Times*, August 31, 2015.

78. Katherine Morton, *China and the Global Environment*, op. cit., p. 4.

79. See The World Bank, *Addressing China's Water Scarcity* (Washington, DC: International Bank for Reconstruction and Development, 2009).

80. Katherine Morton, *China and the Global Environment*, op. cit., p. 4.

81. See Katherine Morton, "Climate Change and Security at the Third Pole," *Survival* 53: 1 (February-March 2011).

82. Ministry of Environmental Protection of the People's Republic of China, "Laws, Statutes, and Regulations," available at: http://english.sepa.gov.cn/Policies_Regulations/.

83. Stephen Mufson, "China Steps Up, Slowly but Surely," *The Washington Post*, October 24, 2009.

84. Hu Jintao, "Statement at the Opening Plenary Session of the United Nations Summit on Climate Change," *Beijing Review* 44, November 5, 2009, p. 3.

85. No author, "A New Energy Era Begins," *Magazin-Deutschland.de* 2 (2011), p. 10.

86. Lan Lan, "China Takes Ambitious Green Path," *China Daily*, July 1, 2015.

87. See Chico Harlan, "Even A Modest Slowdown in China Sacks the Global Commodities Market," *Washington Post*, August 29, 2015.

88. International Crisis Group, *China's Thirst for Oil* (Seoul and Brussels: International Crisis Group, 2008), p. 3.

89. International Energy Agency, *World Energy Outlook 2008* (Paris: OECD/ IEA, 2008), pp. 93, 102.

Chapter 4

1. See H. Gordon Skilling and Franklin Griffiths, *Interest Groups in Soviet Politics* (Princeton: Princeton University Press, 1970).

2. This term was coined by Franklyn Griffiths in 1971. See Franklyn Griffiths, "A Tendency Analysis of Soviet Policymaking," in H. Gordon Skilling and Franklyn Griffiths (eds.), *Interest Groups in Soviet Politics* (Princeton: Princeton University Press, 1971).

3. Ibid.

4. See *Deng Xiaoping Wenxuan (1975–1982)* [Collected Works of Deng Xiaoping], (Beijing: Renmin chubanshe, 1983), pp. 302–25.

5. See Harry Harding, *China's Second Revolution: Reform After Mao* (Washington, DC: Brookings Institution Press, 1987).

6. For Zhao's background, see David Shambaugh, *The Making of a Premier: Zhao Ziyang's Provincial Career* (Boulder, CO: Westview Press, 1983).

7. Bruce Gilley, "Deng Xiaoping and His Successors," in William A. Joseph (ed.), *Politics in China: An Introduction* (New York: Oxford University Press, 2014), p. 135.

8. *Communique on the Current State of the Ideological Sphere: A Notice*

from the Central Committee of the Communist Party of China's General Office, full translation available at: http://www.chinafile.com/document-9-chinafile-translation. The original Chinese language document is also publicly available.

9. Ibid.

10. David Shambaugh, *China's Communist Party: Atrophy and Adaptation* (Berkeley and Washington, DC: University of California Press and Woodrow Wilson Press, 2008), particularly chapter 4.

11. See Mary Elise Sarotte, *The Collapse: The Accidental Opening of the Berlin Wall* (New York: Basic Books, 2014).

12. This full critique is provided in David Shambaugh, *China's Communist Party: Atrophy and Adaptation*, op. cit., chapter 4.

13. See Richard Baum, "The Fifteenth National Party Congress: Jiang Takes Command?", *The China Quarterly* (March 1998), pp. 141–56.

14. Jiang Zemin, "Hold High the Banner of Deng Xiaoping Theory for All-Around Advancement of the Cause of Building Socialism with Chinese Characteristics Into the 21st Century," report delivered to the 15th National Congress of the Communist Party of China, September 12, 1997, section VI, available at: http://www.bjreview.com/document/txt/2011-03/25/content_363499_10.htm.

15. See David Shambaugh, *China's Communist Party: Atrophy and Adaptation*, op. cit.; Andrew Nathan, "Authoritarian Resilience," *Journal of Democracy* (January 2003), pp. 6–17; Kjeld Erik Brodsgaard and Zheng Yongnian (eds.), *The Chinese Communist Party in Reform* (London: Routledge, 2006).

16. I acknowledge that many Party intellectuals, such as Li Junru and Yu Keping, as well as other senior Party officials such as Wang Huning, contributed to the political reform program, but I believe that Zeng Qinghong was the main driver of it.

17. The *Decision* is available in Central Propaganda Department (ed.), *Dang de Shiliuju Sizhong Quanhui "Jueding"* [The Decision of the 16th Party Congress Fourth Plenary Session] (Beijing: Xuexi chubanshe and Dangjian Duwu chubanshe, 2004); and "Communist Party of China Publishes Key Policy Document on Governance Capability": http://www.english.peopledaily.com.cn/200409/26/eng20040926_158378.html.

18. See Zeng Qinghong, "Jiaqiang dang de zhizheng nengli jianshe de ganglingxing wenzhai" [Programmatic Materials for Strengthening the Party's Ability to Govern], in Central Propaganda Department (ed.), *Dang de Shilu ju Quanhui "Jueding"* [The Decision of the Sixteenth Party Congress Fourth Plenary Session] (Beijing: Xuexi chubanshe he Dangjian duwu chubanshe, 2004).

19. Zeng Qinghong, "Jiaqiang Dang de Zhizheng Nengli Jianshe de Ganglingxing Wenzhai" [Programmatic Materials for Strengthening the Party's Ability to Govern], in CCP Central Propaganda Department (ed.), ibid., p. 36.

20. Ironically, the Fourth Plenum of the Seventeenth Central Committee, which convened in mid-September 2009, issued a very progressive *Decision* that put the official imprimatur on the reforms of the previous decade—but, in retrospect, it reads more like a eulogy. My understanding is that the Party had been preparing the document internally for much of the previous year and had to go ahead with it, although decisions had been made earlier in the year to retrench and crack down.

21. "Wen Jiabao Promises Political Reform in China," *The Daily Telegraph*, October 4, 2010: http://www.telegraph.co.uk/news/worldnews/asia/china/8040534/Wen-Jiabao-promises-political-reform-for-China.html.

22. "China's Wen Jiabao Calls for "Urgent" Political Reform," *The Daily Telegraph*, March 14, 2012: http://www.telegraph.co.uk/news/worldnews/asia/china/9142333/Chinas-Wen-Jiabao-calls-for-urgent-political-reform.html.

23. "China Needs Political Reform to Avert 'Political Tragedy,'" *The Guardian*, March 14, 2012: http://www.theguardian.com/world/2012/mar/14/china-political-reform-wen-jiabao.

24. My sense of this bureaucratic coalition and its preferences derives in large part from discussions I had with numerous individuals in Chinese academic circles, the media and propaganda system, and the military during the winter of 2009-2010 (when I was a resident visiting scholar at the Chinese Academy of Social Sciences).

25. For an extensive description of repression in China today see Sarah Cook, *The Politburo's Predicament: Confronting the Limitations of Chinese Communist Party Repression* (New York: Freedom House, 2015).

26. For profiles of Xi Jinping, see Jonathan Fenby, "What the West Should Know About Xi Jinping, China's Most Powerful Leader Since Mao," *New Statesman*, June 23, 2015; Evan Osnos, "Born Red," *The New Yorker*, April 6, 2015; Willy Wo-Lap Lam, *Chinese Politics in the Era of Xi Jinping* (London: Routledge, 2015).

27. Graham Allison and Robert D. Blackwill, with Ali Wyne, *Lee Kuan Yew: The Grand Master's Insights on China, the United States, and the World* (Cambridge, MA: MIT Press for the Belfer Center for Science and International Affairs, 2012), p. 17.

28. Xi Jinping, *The Governance of China* (Beijing: Foreign Languages Press, 2014).

29. See Christopher Johnson and Scott Kennedy, "China's Un-Separation of Powers: The Blurred Lines of Party and Government," *Foreign Affairs* (July/August 2015).

30. Sources: "Briefing on China's Anti-Corruption Campaign," CCP International Department briefing March 25, 2015; N.A., "The Devil, or Mr. Wang," *The Economist*, March 28, 2015; David Lague, Benjamin Kang, and Charlie Zhu, "Special Report: Fear and Retribution in Xi's Anti-Corruption Purge," Reuters, December 23, 2014; Yin Pumin, "War on Graft," *Beijing Review*, March 12, 2015.

31. See David Shambaugh, "The Reformers Cometh? Don't Bet on It," *Washington Post*, November 16, 2012.

32. *Documents of the Fourth Plenary Session of the 18th Central Committee of the Communist Party of China* (Beijing: Central Compilation and Translation Press, 2015).

33. Ibid, p. 9.

34. Stanley Lubman, "After Crackdown on Rights Lawyers, China's Legal Reform Path Uncertain," *Wall Street Journal*, "China Realtime" Blog, July 31, 2015: http://blogs.wsj.com/chinarealtime/2015/07/31/after-crackdown-on-rights-lawyers-chinas-legal-reform-path-uncertain/.

35. Donald Clarke, "China's Legal System and the Fourth Plenum," *Asia Policy* 20 (July 2015), p. 14.

36. Ibid., p. 13.

37. See David Lague, Benjamin Kang, and Charlie Zhu, "Special Report: Fear and Retribution in Xi's Anti-Corruption Purge," op. cit.

38. For a broader set of alternatives, see David Shambaugh, "International

Perspectives on the Communist Party of China," *China: An International Journal* (August 2012), pp. 8–22; You Wei (pseud.), "The End of Reform in China: Authoritarian Adaptation Hits the Wall," *Foreign Affairs* (May/June 2015); Cheng Li, "The End of the CCP's Resilient Authoritarianism? A Tripartite Assessment of Shifting Power in China," *The China Quarterly* (September 2012), pp. 595–623.

39. For a fuller description see David Shambaugh, *China's Communist Party: Atrophy and Adaptation*, op cit., chapter 2; Kenneth Jowitt, *New World Disorder: The Leninist Extinction* (Berkeley: University of California Press, 1992); Chalmers Johnson (ed.), *Change in Communist Systems* (Stanford: Stanford University Press, 1970); Zbigniew Brzezinski, *The Grand Failure: The Birth and Death of Communism* (New York: Charles Scribners Sons, 1989); Samuel P. Huntington and Clement H. Moore (eds.), *Authoritarian Politics in Modern Society* (New York: Basic Books, 1970); Richard Lowenthal, "The Ruling Party in a Mature Society," in Mark G. Field (ed.), *Social Consequences of Modernization in Communist Societies* (Baltimore: Johns Hopkins University Press, 1976); Steven Saxonberg, *The Fall: A Comparative Study of the End of Communism* (Amsterdam: Harwood Academic Publishers, 2001); Edwin A. Winckler (ed.), *Transition From Communism in China: Institutional and Comparative Analyses* (Boulder: Lynne Reinner, 1999); Andrew G. Walder (ed.), *The Waning of the Communist State* (Berkeley: University of California Press, 1995); Seymour Martin Lipset and Gyorgy Bence, "Anticipations of the Failure of Communism," *Theory & Society* 23 (1994); Andrew G. Walder, "The Decline of Communist Power: Elements of a Theory of Institutional Change," *Theory & Society*, ibid.

40. This paragraph is drawn from my article "The Coming Chinese Crack-Up," *The Wall Street Journal*, March 6, 2015.

41. See http://up.hurun.net/Humaz/201406/20140606132402353.pdf.

42. Translations of this and other essays by Yu can be found in Yu Keping, *Democracy is a Good Thing: Essays on Politics, Society, and Culture in Contemporary China* (Washington, DC: The Brookings Institution Press, 2009).

43. See Shambaugh, "The Coming Chinese Crack-Up," op. cit.

44. See Andrea Kendall-Taylor and Erica Frantz, "How Autocracies Fall," *The Washington Quarterly* (Spring 2014), pp. 35–47.

Chapter 5

1. In President Xi Jinping's words in a speech to the November 30, 2014 Foreign Affairs Work Conference: "We have advocated the building of a new type of international relations underpinned by win-win cooperation, put forward and followed a policy of upholding justice and pursuing shared interests, and championed a new vision featuring common, comprehensive, cooperative, and sustainable security." Xinhua News Agency, "Xi Eyes More Enabling International Environment for China's Peaceful Development," November 30, 2014.

2. See Wenwen Shen, *China and Its Neighbors: Troubled Relations* (Brussels: EU-Asia Center, 2012): http://www.eu-asiacentre.eu/pub_details.php?pub_id=46; Philip C. Saunders, "China's Role in Asia: Attractive or Assertive?" in David Shambaugh and Michael Yahuda (eds.), *International Relations of Asia* (Lanham, MD: Rowman & Littlefield, 2014, second edition).

3. Office of the Secretary of Defense, *Annual Report to Congress: Military and Security Developments Involving the People's Republic of China 2015* (Washington, DC: United States Department of Defense, 2015), p. 60.

4. See, for example, Phoak Kung, "Cambodia-China Relations: Overcoming the Trust Deficit," *The Diplomat*, October 7, 2014: http://thediplomat.com/2014/10/cambodia-china-relations-overcoming-the-trust-deficit/.

5. Personal impressions from a visit and discussions in New Zealand in July 2014.

6. See Smruti S. Pattanaik, "Controversy Over Chinese Investment in Sri Lanka," *East Asian Forum*, June 5, 2015: http://www.eastasiaforum.org/2015/06/05/controversy-over-chinese-investment-in-sri-lanka/.

7. For an excellent assessment of the new AIIB, see Daniel Bob, Tobias Harris, Masahiro Kawai, and Yun Sun, *Asian Infrastructure Investment Bank: China as Responsible Stakeholder?* (Washington, DC: Sasakawa Peace Foundation, 2015).

8. I am grateful to Robert Sutter on this point.

9. Graham Allison and Robert D. Blackwill, *Lee Kuan Yew: The Grand Master's Insights on China, the United States, and the World* (Cambridge, MA: MIT Press for the Belfer Center for Science & International Affairs, 2012), pp. 6–7.

10. The State Council Information Office of the People's Republic of China, *China's Military Strategy* (May 2015): http://www.china.org.cn/china/2015-05/26/content 35661433.htm. Also see Peter A. Dutton and Ryan D. Martinson (eds.), *Beyond the Wall: Chinese Far Seas Operations* (Newport, Rhode Island: U.S. Naval War College China Maritime Studies Institute, May 2015).
11. See David Shambaugh, *China Goes Global: The Partial Power* (New York and Oxford: Oxford University Press, 2013).
12. Graham Allison, "Avoiding Thucydides' Trap," *Financial Times*, August 22, 2012.
13. Joseph Nye, *Is the American Century Over?* (Cambridge: Polity Press, 2015), p. 67.
14. Quoted from ibid.
15. See Roy Kamphausen, David Lai, and Andrew Scobell (eds.), *The PLA at Home and Abroad: Assessing the Operational Capabilities of China's Military* (Carlisle, PA: U.S. Army War College Strategic Studies Institute, 2010).
16. This is the central argument of my *China Goes Global*, op. cit. Others who agree with this perspective are Jonathan Fenby, *Will China Dominate the 21st Century?* (Cambridge: Polity Press, 2014); Mel Gurtov, *Will This Be China's Century? A Skeptic's View* (Boulder, CO: Lynne Reinner Publishers, 2013); Joseph Nye, *The Future of Power* (New York: Public Affairs, 2011); Regina M. Abrami, William C. Kirby, F. Warren McFarlan, *Can China Lead? Reaching the Limits of Power and Growth* (Cambridge, MA: Harvard Business School Press, 2014).
17. See David Shambaugh, "The Illusion of Chinese Power," *The National Interest*, July 25, 2014: http://nationalinterest.org/feature/the-illusion-chinese-power-10739.
18. David Shambaugh, *Beautiful Imperialist: China Perceives America, 1972-1990* (Princeton: Princeton University Press, 1991).
19. W.I. Thomas, *The Child in America* (New York: Knopf, 1928), p. 572.
20. See David Shambaugh (ed.) *Tangled Titans: The United States & China*, op. cit. This paragraph is drawn from chapter 1.
21. Simon Denyer, "Foreign Firms Fear a Nationalist China," *Washington Post*, September 8, 2015; US-China Business Council 2015 China Business Environment Member Survey: https://www.uschina.org/reports/uscbc-2015-member-company-survey.

22. For an excellent survey of this discourse see Harry Harding, "Has U.S. China Policy Failed?" *The Washington Quarterly* (October 2015).

23. See Gordon H. Chang, *Fateful Ties: A History of America's Preoccupation with China* (Cambridge, MA: Harvard University Press, 2015).

24. See Richard A Bitzinger, "China's Double-Digit Defense Growth: What it Means for a Peaceful Rise," *Foreign Affairs*, March 19, 2015: https://www.foreignaffairs.com/articles/china/2015-03-19/chinas-double-digit-defense-growth. China now has the world's second highest defense budget ($145 billion in 2015). This is the official figure—experts believe real total spending is anywhere from 5 to 25 percent higher.

25. See Michael Pillsbury, *The Hundred Year Marathon: China's Secret Strategy to Replace America as the Global Superpower* (New York: Henry Holt & Co., 2015).

26. Henry Kissinger, *On China* (New York: Penguin Books, 2012).

27. For further details of this debate see my description in *China Goes Global*, op. cit., pp.83–86.

28. See, for example, Bobo Lo, "A Partnership of Convenience," *International New York Times*, June 8, 2012, and his book *Axis of Convenience: Moscow, Beijing, and the New Geopolitics* (London and Washington, DC: Chatham House and The Brookings Institution Press, 2008); Jane Perlez and Neil MacFarquhar, "Rocky Economy Tests Friendship of Xi and Putin," *New York Times*, September 4, 2015.

29. For an comprehensive study of China-EU relations, see David Shambaugh, Eberhard Sandschneider, and Zhou Hong (eds.), *China-Europe Relations: Perceptions, Policies, and Prospects* (London: Routledge, 2008); Katinka Barysch with Charles Grant and Mark Leonard, *Embracing the Dragon: The EU's Partnership with China* (London: Center for European Reform, 2005).

30. European Commission, *China-Europe: Closer Partners, Growing Responsibilities; Competition and Partnership: A Policy for EU-China Trade and Investment*. See http://ec.europa.eu/comm/external_relations/china/docs/06-10-24_final_com.pdf.

31. Francois Godement and John Fox, *A Power Audit of EU-China Relations* (London: European Council on Foreign Relations, 2009), available at: http://ecfr.eu/page/-/documents/A_Power_Audit_of_EU_China_Relations.pdf.

32. Interview with Ambassador Serge Abou, Delegation of the European Union, February 4, 2010, Beijing.

33. European Commission, "Trade in Goods with China (2014)": http://trade.ec.europa.eu/doclib/docs/2006/september/tradoc_113366.pdf.

34. "European Investment in Europe Reaches Record High in 2014": http://www.bakermckenzie.com/news/Chinese-investment-into-Europe-hits-record-high-in-2014-02-11-2015/.

35. Gill Plimmer and Lucy Hornsby, "China to Invest £105 Bn. in UK Infrastructure by 2025," *Financial Times*, October 27, 2014.

36. See European Chamber of Commerce, *European Business in China: Business Confidence Survey* (Beijing: European Chamber in partnership with Roland Berger Strategy Consultants, 2015).

37. See Parke Nicolson, "The Beijing-Berlin Connection: How China and Europe Forged Stronger Ties," *Foreign Affairs*, August 13, 2015: https://www.foreignaffairs.com/articles/china/2015-08-13/beijing-berlin-connection.

38. See Erik Voeten and Adis Merdzanovic, *United Nations General Assembly Voting Data*, available at: http://hdl:1901.1/12379UNF:3Hpf6qOkDdzzvX F9m66yLTg=.html.

39. Information Office of the State Council, *China's Foreign Aid* (April 2011): http://news.xinhuaneet.com/english2010/china/2011-04/21/C_13839683.htm.

40. International Energy Agency, *World Energy Outlook 2008* (Paris: OECD/IEA, 2008), pp. 93, 102.

41. N.A., "One of Many: China Has Become Big in Africa, Now for the Backlash," *The Economist*, January 17, 2015; Howard French, *China's Second Continent: How a Million Migrants are Building a New Empire in Africa* (New York: Knopf, 2014).

42. Pew Research Center, "America's Global Image Remains More Positive than China's," July 18, 2013: http://www.pewglobal.org/2013/07/18/chapter-1-attitudes-toward-the-united-states/.

43. See David Shambaugh, "China's Soft-Power Push," *Foreign Affairs* (July/August 2015).

44. Richard A. Bitzinger, "China's Double-Digit Defense Growth," *Foreign Affairs*, March 19, 2015: https://www.foreignaffairs.com/articles/china/2015-03-19/chinas-double-digit-defense-growth.

45. The State Council Information Office of the People's Republic of China, *China's Military Strategy* (May 2015), op. cit., p. 8.

46. A particularly good study of the future of China's military is Roy Kamphausen and David Lai (eds.), *The Chinese People's Liberation Army in 2025* (Carlisle, PA: U.S. Army War College Strategic Studies Institute, 2015).

47. Yin Pumin, "War on Graft," *Beijing Review*, March 12, 2015.

48. See G. John Ikenberry, "The Rise of China, the United States, and the Future of the Liberal International Order," in David Shambaugh (ed.), *Tangled Titans: The United States & China* (Lanham, MD: Rowman & Littlefield, 2013).

49. See David Shambaugh, *China Goes Global: The Partial Power* (New York and Oxford: Oxford University Press, 2013), chapter 4; David Shambaugh, "Coping with a Conflicted China," *The Washington Quarterly* (Winter 2011); Michael Fullilove, *The Stakeholder Spectrum: China and the United Nations* (Sydney: Lowy Institute for International Policy, 2010).

Index